FORENSIC SCIENCE
AND
CRIME INVESTIGATION

FORENSIC SCIENCE AND CRIME INVESTIGATION

Chief Editor:
RAMESH CHANDRA
Editors:
SURINDER NATH • P.K. JANJUA

ABHIJEET PUBLICTIONS
DELHI 110 094

ABHIJEET PUBLICATIONS
2/46 Tukhmeerpur Extension
Delhi-110 094
Phone: 2218 1492
e-mails: abhijeet_singh@vsnl.net
abhijeet_singh1@indiatimes.com

FORENSIC SCIENCE AND CRIME INVESTIGATION

First Published 2005
Revised Edition 2020

ISBN 81-88683-60-4

₹ 750/-

PRINTED IN INDIA

Published by J.K. Singh for Abhijeet Publications, Delhi 110 094; Lasertypeset by Rajesh Data Services, New Delhi, and Printed at Tarun Offset Press, Delhi.

Preface

Forensic science encompasses a wide variety of scientific disciplines. Its foremost purpose is to offer unprejudiced, scientific support for use in courts of law. Scientific analysis of physical evidence is compulsory to assist the police in their investigations. These examinations include—detection of blood, semen, saliva, and other body fluids. Blood grouping from dried blood, or semen stains. Determination of origin of species from blood stains. Use of DNA profiling to compare the unidentified samples for the purpose of identification.

Identification of trace elements like— fibers, hair (site and origin of species). Recognition and analysis of blood and urine samples in cases of consumption of drugs and alcohol in offences like driving under the effect of intoxication, or in cases of poisoning. Examination of glass fragments and paint samples by means of microscopic techniques as well as physical and chemical methods. Examination and analysis of skeletal material, intact or in fragmentary state, recovered from crime scenes to establish identity in terms of establishing age, sex, race, and stature, etc.

Scientists work closely with police and on certain occasions they may even have to visit the scene of crime to get certain relevant information about the crime. The forensic scientists often give evidence in the court, which may be of great use.

Bundelkhand University, Jhansi initiated a teaching programme in Forensic science, a much sought for teaching programme in the present day context. Forensic science as a subject is gaining recognition day by day and as a consequence more and more Universities are including this subject in their teaching curriculum.

The Institute of Forensic Science and Criminology, Bundelkhand University organized a National Conference on The Role of Forensic Science in Crime Investigation during February 13-14, 2002. The National Conference was the first ever in the State of Uttar Pradesh and was well attended by the practicing Forensic Scientists from all over India.

This volume is an outcome of the National Conference and has a total of twenty research papers pertaining to various aspects of Forensic Science.

Out of the twenty-one research papers three each pertain to examination of Questioned Documents, Modern Techniques used in performing identification through fingerprints and on Reconstruction of Stature from long bone lengths of living population groups of India. Two articles each follow these on Drug Abuse, Crime against Women and on Exhumation and Departed Soul. Lastly, the volume includes on article each on Role of DNA Fingerprinting, Ballistics, Comparative examination of eruption pattern of third molar, White Collar Crime—an unperceived area of crime and finally of Forensic Entomology (this is perhaps an important area of crime and finally on Forensic Entomology). This is perhaps an important area of forensic science but least worked as no database is yet available in India.

This book would be useful to Forensic Scientists working in State and Central Forensic Science Laboratories across the country as well as to the Law Institutes, Police administration, Fingerprint Bureau, Question Document Examiners and Chemical Examiners. This volume would be of great use in all University/College departments where Forensic Science and or Criminology is taught as a discipline at any level—Certificate, Diploma or Degree. In Medical Colleges this book would be of great use to the teachers and students of Forensic Medicine. This book would be quite handy for the practicing lawyers to prepare their cases.

Editors

Contents

Preface v

1. Role of DNA Fingerprinting in Forensic Science 1
   — *Anupama Raina & T.D. Dogra*
2. Exhumation—Plugging of Pitfalls 5
   — *Dr. Adarsh Kumar & Dr. Krishan Vij*
3. Spasma-Proxyvon Drug Abuse—An Enzymatic Study 11
   — *M.I. Shah, H.S. Maheshwari & S.K. Jain*
4. Women Victimization 16
   — *A. Panwar, P.K. Janjua & N.K. Kanwal*
5. Regression Analysis of Penetration Data on Window Pane and It's Impact Energy by Indian Made Soft Nose Bullet 23
   — *N.P. Waghmare, M.S. Rao, A. Manna, A.K. Pal & S.S. Badwal*
6. A Preliminary Report on Class Characteristics of Handwriting in School Children 32
   — *V. Roshan, B. Verma, N.K. Kanwal & P.K. Janjua*
7. White Collar Crime—An Unperceived Area of Crime 38
   — *Pallavi Gupta*
8. Reconstruction of Stature from Upper Extremity Bone Lengths 49
   — *Surinder Nath*

9. Study of Physical Dependence of Chronic Pentazocine Administered Albino Rats — *M.I. Shah, H.S. Maheshwari & S.K. Jain* 64

10. Crimes Against Women and Role of Forensic Science — *Bindu Variath* 72

11. Forensic Importance of Insects Sequentially Colonizing Carcasses — *Devinder Singh & Meenakshi Bharti* 80

12. Pattern Recognition — *Yashpal Singh, Aditya Chaturvedi, Priyank Tripathi & Ankur Katiyar* 89

13. Fingerprint Matching — *Yashpal Singh & Priyank Tripathi* 97

14. Is Perfect Forgery Possible? — *S.K. Saxena* 105

15. History and Development of Fingerprints Identification System: A Review Paper — *P.K. Janjua, N.K. Kanwal, R.K. Garg & Surinder Nath* 107

16. A Study on Eruption of Third Molar of the Jat Sikhs and Muslims of Punjab — *A. Singla, P.K. Janjua, & N.K. Kanwal* 125

17. Prediction of Stature through Hand and Foot Lengths among Brahmins of Himachal Pradesh — *Surinder Nath, Divya Chugh, Renu Rani & Bhavna* 140

18. Formulation of Multiplication Factors for Estimation of Stature Using Upper Extremity Dimensions Among Male and Female Tangkhul Nagas of Manipur — *L. Sunita Devi & Surinder Nath* 150

19. Reconstruction of Stature Among Jains of Delhi through Lower Limb Dimensions — *Surinder Nath, Preeti Jain, & Bhavna* 158

20. Executant Genuine But Agreement Forged — *Vikram Raj Singh Chauhan* 168

21. Can the Departed Soul Be Lived Again — *Vikram Raj Singh Chauhan* 174

1

Role of DNA Fingerprinting in Forensic Science

*Anupama Raina**
*T.D. Dogra***

The advent of modern DNA technology, the technique widely preferred in the field of Forensic Science has resulted in the increased ability to perform human identity testing, DNA fingerprinting is also often referred to "DNA genetic pattern" as it determines DNA pattern from an individuals genetic materials and is as authentic as Fingerprints (Dactylograph).

An average human being has approximately trillion cell namely blood cells, muscle cells, skin cells and so forth. And each cell has a number of components like Golgi complex, ribosome etc., but the genetic material resides in the chromosomes located in the nucleus. Within the nucleus of the cells is a chemical substance known as De-oxy-ribonucleic Acid (DNA), hence referred as nuclear DNA. DNA, the genetic material stores the information necessary for passing down genetic attributes to future generations. Since DNA resides in every cell, it provides a program that determines the physical features and many other attributes of an individual.

* Department of Forensic Medicine & Toxicology, AIIMS, New Delhi.

The discovery of DNA was mainly focused in 1980 by Watson and Crick. The structure designed by them was based on X-ray diffraction studies. DNA is composed of Nucleotide unit and each unit has:

(*a*) De-oxyribose (sugar)

(*b*) Phosphate

(*c*) Nucleolase

Sugar and Phosphate forms the backbone of DNA while nucleobase imparts variation in each nucleotide unit. There are four (4) nucleobases (Thymine, Cytosine, Guanine and Adenine) and it is the combination of these four, known as nucleotide which yields the diverse biological differences and human beings and all living creatures. Humans have approximately 3 billion nucleotide positions in the total genomic DNA. With four possibilities at each position, literally trillions of combination are possible.

DNA consists of two single strands which are linked together through a process called "hybridization". Hybridization of two strands is a fundamental property of DNA. However, the hydrogen bonds holding the two strands of DNA together through base pairing may be broken at increased temperature or by chemical treatment known as "denaturation". These two single strands form a double helix due to base-pairing phenomenon: The base pairing rules are such that Adenine can only hybridize to Thymine and Cytosine can only hybridize to Guanine. These bases are attached to each other by hydrogen bonds.

The DNA material in chromosomes is composed of 'coding' and non-coding regions. The coding regions are known as "Genes" and it contains information necessary for a cell to make proteins. Genes consists of exons and introns and make up 5% of human genomic DNA. Rest 95% of DNA is referred as Junk DNA because its function is not fully known. Surprisingly, it is this Junk DNA which shows variability among individuals. The location of gene in a non-coding region is commonly referred to as a *locus* (plura: *loci*) and the alternative possibilities for a gene or genetic locus are termed *alleles*. If the two alleles at a genetic locus on homologous chromosomes are different, they are termed as *heterozygous* and if the alleles are identical at a particular locus, they are termed as *homozygous.* Heterozygous and homozygous positions at corresponding loci are essential to human identity testing.

The concept of DNA fingerprinting was introduced by Prof. Alec Jefferys in 1985 and general public has become more familiar with the power of DNA typing these days as the media has projected the cases of Ex-president of US, Clinton-Monica Lewinsky and O.J. Simpson. Dr. Jeffreys found that certain regions of DNA contained DNA sequences that were repeated over the over again next to each other which are referred as VNTR. In addition, he also discovered that the number of repeated sequences present in a sample could differ from individual to individual. It is considered as the most powerful tool to identify an individual. Earlier an individual was identified using some conventional techniques like, ABO, MNs, Rh etc. blood groups and serum proteins etc. but now DNA fingerprinting is preferred because DNA is much more resistant to the degradation caused by the environment conditions. Moreover, DNA is somatically stable. This uniqueness of DNA forms the basis of DNA fingerprinting which is based on Mandelian law of inheritance.

Eukaryotic genomes are full or repeated DNA sequences. These repeated DNA sequences come in all types of sizes and are designated by the core repeat unit. These regions are often referred as satellite DNA, which is classified into:

(a) Minisatellite DNA

(b) Microsatellite DNA

Microsatellites are also referred as Short Tandem Repeats (STR's). These STR's are scattered throughout the genome and occur on average every 10000 nucleotides. STR markers have an advantage that they can be analysed using multiplex Polymerase Chain reaction (PCR). PCR technique is mostly preferred these days because DNA recovered form most of the biological samples sent for DNA analysis is very less. Using earlier DNA technique (radioactive one) about 10-20 ng of DNA is essential whereas for PCR technique even few micro grams DNA is sufficient. One of the main advantage of multiplex PCR is that an individual can be analysed at several loci simultaneously. It also consumes very less time. It is an ideal technique for DNA typing because the probability of identical alleles in 2 individual decreases with an increase in the number of polymorphic loci. Ideal STR's for forensic purpose should combine characteristics such as hypervariability, low mutation rate, robustness, low stutter characteristics and small size.

This revolutionary novel method to identify an individual has main applications in:

(1) Criminal cases

 Rape

 Murder

(2) Civil cases

 Paternity dispute

 Immigration

(3) Plant genetics

(4) Animal genetics

(5) Organ transplantation

DNA fingerprinting as an evidence is very much accepted in the Indian court of law as it proves the identity of an individual with 100% proof.

2

Exhumation – Plugging of Pitfalls

*Dr. Adarsh Kumar**

*Dr. Krishan Vij***

Abstract

Although "Exhumation" (lawful digging--out of already buried dead body), is rarity in our country; yet the CASES have attracted a lot of media attention, whenever it is done. Scientists from all streams of forensic sciences whether it be Anthropologist, Fingerprint Expert, Serologist, Forensic Odontologist or a medical sciences i.e. Forensic Pathologist (doctor); are involved in the procedure along with other agencies like Police & Photographs.

Though and procedure is carried out in the presence of Magistrate & through legal authorization; yet few shortcomings remain due to lack of proper co-ordination amongst these personnel. Lack of team-work concept invariably leads to loss of vital clues and evidences; primarily affecting the interpretation of findings and ultimately the outcome of the case.

* Sr. Lecturer, Department of Forensic Medicine Government Medical College, Sector 32, Chandigarh-160 030.

** Prof. & Head, Department of Forensic Medicine, Government Medical College, Sector 32, Chandigarh-160 030.

Some policy for carrying-out the procedure with team-work concept, is the need of the hour, which will adequately plug these pitfalls. The paper describes the procedure/protocol to be adopted/followed in such cases, incorporating latest technological advances made in the field of criminal investigation all over the globe which will assist in better disbursement of justice.

Key Words: Forensic Science, Forensic Scientists, Exhumation, Recent Advances

Introduction

Exhumation i.e. Retrieval of previously buried dead body practically speaking, is uncommon in our country, due to custom of cremation prevalent amongst Hindus which constitute the larger portion of the population. However, in other communities who practice burial of the dead body, exhumation can be done, if any controversy regarding identity, cause or manner of death arises afterwards.

Another situation observed in medico-legal practice is *'buried-body'* cases, which come to attention of police either as an accidental finding or during the course of confession by a criminal or provided by an informant. Rarely the second autopsy may be required when first postmortem report is challenged by public or due to political over tones.

In our set up, as soon as information reaches the police, they rush to the site and start their procedural formalities; although Section 176 CrPC requires authorization and presence of First Class Magistrate. This rushing disturbs the *'preservation of scene'* which is of paramount importance in all such cases. Doctors are usually called later and Forensic Scientists rarely, creating total lack of co-ordination among themselves which ultimately lead to loss of many vital evidences at the site/scene and during the process; the importance of those can be understood by these personnel only. Following procedure is recommended to plug these pitfalls in the existing process with incorporation of latest technological advances made in the field of science.

Recommended Procedure

Preliminary phase of any investigation is most critical and it sets the tune for whole of the investigation. Conducting site/scene search involving discovery & excavation of buried bodies requires special technique & planning. Team-work concept must be developed for better results. The doctor preferably a medicolegist along with Forensic Scientists viz. Forensic Anthropologist, Forensic Entomologist, Forensic Serologist, Forensic Animator & other specialized personnel like Photographer, Finger print Expert; must be made the integral part of the team. This team should be involved right from the beginning of the process along with Police & Magistrate.

At the site, immediate excavation of remains must not be done, if the body has not already been removed. Entire area must be cordoned off & any access to public must be denied, which can be done by using tarpaulin screen around the site. After securing the area, the preliminary procedure should be instituted in the following manner.

A. Preliminaries

1. *Photographer* must take both black & white and coloured photographs of entire area including the site and any item of evidentiary value first.
2. The area surrounding the site should be mapped-out & a scene sketch i.e. plan view be prepared by Specialized personnel like portraitist/sketcher/*Forensic Animator* after proper scaling.
3. A systematic search of surrounding area invites special attention. If any evidence is discovered, it is to be photographed separately & included on scene sketch.
4. Fingerprints need be lifted from all possible evidences.
5. Always carry out the procedure in daylight preferably during early morning hours and if rainy weather is a threat, protect the area/site by erecting the tents.

B. Exhumation Proper

1. When the grave is identified by relative & cemetery in-charge; the problem of locating the site does not arise. However it poses a great deal of difficulty in *'buried-body'* cases & as such may involve several acre areas to be dug out. For locating the burial site, following can be of great help:

   (a) Circumstances of crime which may give a clue

   (b) Search by foot

   (c) *Probing*—steel rod 4-5 feet long with tee handle on one end and a sharp point at other is inserted into suspected area; if ground is soft it is halted & vapour detector is brought into play.

   (d) *Vapour Detector*—detects presence of gases formed as a result of decomposition and so can detect the presence of cadaver.

2. Clearing of the ground around burial site is of critical value for exactly locating the dimension of hole to be followed by photography.

3. The soil should be scrapped-off in somewhat even layers about 4"-6" deep. As various evidences are located & recovered, they should be photographed.

   During digging-out, the soil samples warrants to be collected from near the grave, around the grave, over the grave & as different items/evidences are recovered preferably by a *Forensic Geologist* a handful of soil needs to be gathered from each location, dried before packaging in different containers with proper identification. The containers must be clean, dry & wide-mouthed.

4. *Forensic Botanist & Forensic Geotaphonomist* (who deals with buried crime scene evidences) should collect the surface vegetation & roots of tree and bushes which have grown into the site & the remains.

5. Photography of grave is of utmost importance as soon as coffin or body is visualized, prior to any disturbance, which should be identified by as much person as possible

present at the site. The doctor should examine dead body inside the grave & later conduct preliminary autopsy then & there, if body has intact soft tissue. *Forensic Entomologist* should collect various insects/ larvae & other evidences at this juncture, which will help him in extending his expert opinion.

6. The body may then be placed on a clean, white sheet for better visualization & preservation of any additional evidence, which may not be easily observable at site.

   The importance of collection & preservation of soil samples from around the body and underneath it, in actual contact; can not be over-emphasized. A portion of coffin & buried clothes, scalp & public hairs & viscera, if identifiable; should also be preserved.

7. After removing the body, the grave should again be photographed. Area under the body invites careful searching for any teeth, hyoid bone, thyroid cartilage & bullets; followed by further excavation for several inches. Use of *metal detector* at this stage will certainly yield better results.

8. The hands of the deceased should be bagged with paper bags for preservation of any trace evidence under fingernails. The body afterwards be transported to nearest mortuary for further examination & detailed autopsy.

   Forensic Anthropologist & *Forensic Odontologist* may be involved, if body is in highly decomposed state.

Conclusion

Teamwork concept is hallmark for all the phases of investigation to yield better results. It requires an appreciation & understanding of each other's duties & responsibilities; so that all parties can benefit from one another's contribution & expertise.

Proper retrieval of physical evidence needs a very careful handling & it is this part which is lacking most. All the personnel involved must have working knowledge of handling the physical evidence. *Anything & everything can be evidence, so ALWAYS PRESERVE, if not absolutely sure as useless.*

Thorough packaging & labelling of collected material & further proper storage & transmission is very crucial in maintaining *'Chain of Evidence'* which ultimately has the bearing on the outcome of the case.

In this modern era of technological spin-off, few such things may be used as an adjunct or alternative depending upon expertise exhibited. In addition to photography, *videography* may also be done as it provides a realistic & graphic portrayal of the scene, which can be reviewed also by all concerned. However, technique of videography is crucial in determining it's evidentiary value.

Another is *'Total Station System'*, which is an electronic measuring equipment developed for taking scene measurements. It records distance, slope, horizontal & vertical angle to a given point. The system may substitute measuring tapes, sketches, diagrams etc. in future, as it saves the countless hours of manpower consumed at scene. Other advantage of it is in making 3-dimensional views & animated reconstruction, which can easily be done with the help of Auto CAD on the Computer.

The recommended protocol, we sincerely hope will enhance the role of all categories of Forensic Scientist in the process of Criminal Investigation and ultimately benefit the society by helping in better disbursement of justice.

3

Spasma-Proxyvon Drug Abuse – An Enzymatic Study

*M.I. Shah**

*H.S. Maheshwari***

*S.K. Jain****

Abstract

Spasma-proxyvon (SP) is an anti-spasma drug which is therapeutically used for the treatment of severe colic pain. It has been reported that, the spasma-prozyvon capsule is being used for alteration of mood by drug abusers.

The present work has been planned to study the hepatotoxicity of spasma-proxyvon in albino rats. For the purpose, two groups of albino rats, each group comprising of 10 animals were chosen. Group first was kept as control, whereas second group was administered with spasma-proxyvon capsule. The dose was 1.50 mg 100 gm[1] body weight (>ED50) twice a day for seven days after completion of drug

* Dr. H.S. Gour University, Sagar. (India)

** Dr. H.S. Gour University, Sagar. (India)

*** Dr. H.S. Gour University, Sagar. (India)

treatment period, the blood was collected for estimation of serum enzymes GOT and GPT level.

The SP treated albino rats showed a significant increase in the level of serum transferase enzymes. It clearly indicates that SP produce hepatic injury, if used regularly with large dose.

Introduction

People in every society are using drugs that effect on mood, thoughts and feeling since as back as recorded history.

These drugs varied from classical drugs viz., opium, cannabis etc. to the modern synthetic drugs such as LSD, amphetamine, heroin etc. The choice of these drugs varies from time to time amongst drug abusers.

Amongst these abusive drugs Spasma Proxiyron (SP) is a latest choice of drug abusers. Spasma-proxyvon is an anti-spasma drug which is used for the treatment of severe colic pain but today it is widely abused in India, mainly in North-Eastern States. The spasma-proxyvon is popularly known as SP and is available either as capsule or injectible form in the market.

Spasma-Proxyvon

The capsule and injectible form of spasma-proxyvon have the following composition.

Composition of a Spasma-Proxyvon Capsule

Content	*Amount*	*Effect*
Dicyclomine HCL	10 mg.	Anti-spasma
Dixtopropoxyphene HCL	65 mg.	Analgesic opioid (Codeine like effect)
Acetaminophen	400 mg.	Analgesic-antipyretic (also called coalter analgesic)

Composition of a Spasma-Proxyvon Injection

Content	*Amount*	*Effect*
Dicyclomine HCL	10 mg.	Anti-spasma
Diclofenac Sodium	65 mg.	Anti-inflammatory

Propoxyphene binds to opioid receptors and produces analgesia and other CNS effect (e.g. hallucination, sedation and drowsiness etc.) similar to those seen with codein and other opioids. It is an abusive drug so, it has been placed in Schedule IV, of the Federal Controlled Substances Act 1971 in the United States (Jasinski et al, 1977; Goodman and Gilman, 1985). But the SP has not been included in the list of schedule II of Narcotic drugs and Psychotropic Substances Act 1985 of India. Hence, it is available without prescription in the open market.

The SP capsule becomes abused due to the presence of abusive drugs i.e. propoxyphene and acetaminophena in it.

Experimental

For the study, two groups of albino rats, each group comprising of 10 animals were selected. Group first was kept as control, whereas second group was orally administration SP capsule in the dose of 1.50 mg 100 gm[1] body weight twice a day for seven days. This dose is more than twice of ED_{50}, because the drug abusers usually take large dose of SP. Later on the blood was collected for thc estimation of the Serum Glutamate Oxaloacetate Transferase (SGOT) and Serum Glutamate Phyuvate Transferase (SGPT) enzymes by Reitman-Frankel method. (Pillai and Qudry, 1966).

Results

The results of transferase enzymes in both control and SP treated rats has been summarized in Table 1.

Table 1

N = 10

Enzyme	*Transferase enzymes (SF unit/dl.of blood)*	
	Control animals	*Drug treated animals*
SGOT	18.28 ± 1.50	24.12 ± 1.22 P*
SGPT	16.91 ± 1.29	22.60 ± 1.32 P*

P* Significant at $P < 0.05$, df=18.

Discussion

Table 1 shows the level of transferase enzymes in both control and SP capsule treated group of albino rats. The drug administered group of rats have shown a significant increase of SGOT and SGPT level. Goodman and Gilman (1985) elucidated that, acetaminophen produces significant elevation of serum transferases.

Ameer and Greebablt (1977), Prescott and Critchley (1983), Parikh (1996) have mentioned that paracetamol (acetaminophen) produces hepatic necrosis in both man and animal. It is probably due to the elevation of cytosolic free Ca^{+2} (Moore et al, 1985 and Shen et al, 1992) which causes a decrease of covalent binding to microsomal proteins (Holtzman, 1995).

Conclusions

From the study it is concluded that the SP capsule may produce hepatic necrosis due to the presence of strong hepatotoxic agent i.e., acetaminophen (paracetamol) in large quantity (400 mg. per capsule). The death of SP abusers as reported in literature may be due to the hepatotoxicity developed by its prolonged usage.

REFERENCES

1. Ameer, B and Greenblat, D.J.; Acctaminophen. *Ann. Intern. Med.* (1977), 87, 202-209.
2. Goodman, G.A. and Gilman, L.S.; *The Pharmacological Basis of Therapeutics*, Macmillan, 7th ed. London (1985), pp. 693-695.
3. Holtzman, J.L; The role of covalent binding to microsomal proteins in the hepatotoxicity of acetaminophe, *Drug Method Rev.* 27:277-297(1995).
4. Jasinski, Dr. et al; Therapeutic usefulness of propoxyphene napsylate in narcotic addictions. *Arch. Gen. Psychiatry.* (1977), 34, pp. 227-233.
5. More, M., Thor, H.O., Moore, G.O., Nelson, O.S. Modeus, O. and Orenius S.; The toxicity of acetaminophen and N-acetyl-p-benzoquinone in isolated hepatocytes associated with thiol depletion and increased cytosolic Ca^{+2}, *J.Biol. Chemi,* 260: 13037-13040 (1985).

6. Parikh, C.K.; *Text Book of Medical Jurisprudence and Toxicology,* CBS Publishers and Distributors Bombay, Reprint (1996) p. 950.
7. Pillai, K.K. and Qadry, J.S.; *Biochemistry and Clinical Pathology,* CBS Publishers and Distributors, Reprint, Delhi (1996).
8. Prescott, L.F. and Critchley, J.A.J.H.; The treatment of acetaminophen poisoning. *Annu. Rev. Pharmacol. Toxico,.* (1983), 23, 87-101.
9. Shen, W.O.; Kamendulis, L.M.O.; Ray, S.D. and Corcoran, G.B.; Acetaminophen-induced cytotoxicity in cultured mouse hepatocytes: effects of Ca endonuclease, DNA repaid and glutathione depletion inhibitions on DNA fragmentation and cell death. *Toxico. Appl. pharmacol.* 112; 32-40 (1992).

4

Women Victimization

*A. Panwar**
*P.K. Janjua***
*N.K. Kanwal****

Abstract

We have got our independence 54 years ago and our constitution say that all citizens of India have equal status and they are equal in the eyes of law but still we find that ours is a male dominant society. Though women victimization was not uncommon in ancient societies but now as we expect that there should be some positive effect of education and civilized society, as is our society, we expect that development of our society. To study this effect F.I. Rs of last 12 years from Distt. Panipat of state Haryana (India) were collected and analyzed and it was found that during the period of 1989-92, cases of women victimization were 2.53% of the total number of crimes

* P .G. Student, Institute of Forensic Science & Criminology, Bundelkhand University, Jhasi.

** Head, Institute of Forensic Science & Criminology, Bundelkhand University, Jhansi.

*** Lecturer, Institute of Forensic Science & Criminology, Bundelkhand University, Jhansi.

which increased to 3.89% during 1993-96 and this percentage further increased to 4.60% during 1997-2000. This study was carried out only in one Distt. of a state showing a gradual increase in women victimization. This needs efforts of various workers for further study.

Introduction

Any act that is against the peace or interest of society is generally called 'Crime' various authors have defined crime as "Any act which is forbidden by Law and revolting to the moral sentiments of society" (STEPHEN) and as "Any act committed or omitted, in violation of public law, either forbidding or commanding it" (BLACK STONE). Thus, it is clear that crime is any antisocial behaviour and injurious to society. We cannot expect any society totally devoid of crime. Even after 54 years of independence and when our constitution has provided equal status to all the citizens of our country, crimes against women are increasing. Though crimes against women were committed in ancient societies also but now we expect that crime rate should decrease because of course civilization and education must have positively effected the fall of crime rate but actually the crime rate against women is increasing despite all possible efforts of Govt. Police, other Govt. Semi-Govt, and private organizations. The present study was carried out for studying the most commonly encountered crimes against women.

Materials and Methods

The present study was conducted in Panipat Distt. of state Haryana (India) for which the matter was discussed with various Police officers and F.I.Rs from all the police stations of District Panipat were studies and data was prepared for crimes reported during the period of 12 years and out of the total number of cases the cases of women victimization where separated out and categorized as follows (alphabetically listed):

(1) Assault & criminal force at women to outrage her modesty.

(2) Abetment of suicide.

(3) Chain snatching.

(4) Dowry death.

(5) Eve teasing.

(6) Harassment for dowry.

(7) Kidnapping and abduction.

(8) Rape.

Results and Discussion

Table 1
Women Victimization during 1989-1992

Sr. No.	*Type of Crime*	*1989*	*1990*	*1991*	*1992*	*Total*
1.	Assault of criminal force to women to outrage her modesty	02	08	07	12	29
2.	Abetment of suicide	00	02	01	05	08
3.	Chain Snatching	01	01	03	09	14
4.	Dowry Death	00	08	05	08	21
5.	Eve Teasing	02	22	17	18	59
6.	Harassment for Dowry	00	05	09	10	24
7.	Kidnapping & abduction	01	06	06	17	30
8.	Rape	01	06	06	17	30

Total No. of case of women victimization during 1989-92=218

Total (1) shows that during the period of 1982-92 total 218 cases of women victimization were recorded of which maximum number was of cases of eve teasing (59)> followed by cases of kidnapping & abduction (33)> rape cases (3)> then cases of assault and criminal force to women to outrage her modesty (29),> dowry harassment cases (24)> dowry death (21) chain snatching (14)> & the minimum number of cases were of abetment of suicide (08).

Table 2
Women victimization during 1993-1996

Sr.No	*Type of Crime*	*1993*	*1994*	*1995*	*1996*	*Total*
1.	Assault of criminal force to women to outrage her modesty	04	12	05	16	37
2.	Abetment of suicide	04	03	04	04	15
3.	Chain snatching	07	11	08	14	40
4.	Dowry death	08	04	12	08	32
5.	Eve teasing	26	28	27	22	103
6.	Harassment for dowry	07	20	16	19	62
7.	Kidnapping & abduction	06	07	06	12	41
8.	Rape	08	08	23	13	62

Total number of cases of women victimization during 1993-96=392

From Table (2) it is evident that during 1993-96 out of a total of 392, again cases of eve teasing were maximum in number (101). But here on second place are the cases of rape (62) & harassment for dowry (62)> followed by cases of kidnapping and abduction (41)> closely followed by cases of chain snatching (40)> then the cases of assault and criminal force at women to outrage her modesty (37)> & dowry death (32)> abetment of suicide (15).

Table 3
Women victimization during 1997-2000

Sr. No.	*Type of Crime*	*1997*	*1998*	*1999*	*2000*	*Total*
1.	Assault of criminal force to women to outrage her modesty	15	16	13	17	61
2.	Abetment of suicide	03	01	06	05	15
3.	Chain snatching	06	06	14	16	42
4.	Dowry death	07	12	14	15	48
5.	Eve teasing	22	30	16	21	89
6.	Harassment for dowry	28	66	67	44	205
7.	Kidnapping & abduction	26	07	19	11	63
8.	Rape	15	24	22	34	95

Total Number of cases of women victimization during 1997-2000=618

If we observe the data of Table (3), it shows that out of a total of 618, cases of harassment for dowry were the maximum in number (205) which is comparatively a very huge number> then the cases of rape (95)> eve teasing (89) were recorded which were followed by cases of kidnapping & abduction (63)> Closely followed by cases of assault and criminal force to women to outrage her modesty (61)> dowry death cases (48)> chain snatching (42)> & then the cases of abetment of suicide (15) have their place as in table (1).

Table 4
Comparative Data of Women Victimization during 1989-2000

Sr. No.	*Type of Crime*	*1989-92*	*1993-96*	*1997-2000*
1.	Assault of criminal force to women to outrage her modesty	29	37	61
2.	Abetment of suicide	08	15	15
3.	Chain snatching	14	40	42
4.	Dowry death	21	32	48
5.	Eve teasing	59	103	89
6.	Harassment for dowry	24	62	205
7.	Kidnapping & abduction	33	41	63
8.	Rape	33	62	95
	Total	218	392	618

Total number of cases of women victimization during 1989-2000=1228

From table (4) it is clear that during 1989-92 total 219 cases of women victimization were recorded which increased to 392 during 1993-96 & further the number increased to 618 during 1997-2000.

During 1989-92 the cases which were recorded in maximum number were of eve teasing (59) which increased to 103 during 1993096 but this number decreased to 89 during 1997-2999. On the second place were the cases of kidnapping and abduction (33) during the period of 1989-92 which increased to 41 during 1993-96 and further during 1997-2000 the number increased to 63 showing a gradual increase. At the third place during 1989-92 were the rape cases (33) the number of which increased to 62 during 1993-95 and during 1997-2000. This number further increased to 95 showing an increase of about 30 during each period of 4 years. Similarly the cases of assault and Criminal force to women to outrage her modesty were 29 during 1989-92, increased to 37 during 1993-96 and to 61 during 1997-2000 again showing a gradual increase in number. After this the cases of harassment for dowry were recorded which were 24 during 1989-92, 62 during 1993-96 and a very steep increase was observed during 1997-2000 as the number increased to 205 (whatever may be the reason—either due to education of women or general awareness). Then at the sixth place, cases of dowry death were recorded, the number being 21 during 1989-92, 32 during 1993-96, and further increased to 48 during 1997-2000. The number of cases of chain snatching was 14 during 1989-92 40 during 1993-96 and the number slightly increased during 1997-2000 and reached 42. The minimum number of cases were recorded under the heading 'abetment of suicide' which was during 1989-92, increased to 15 during 1993-96 but unlike all other crimes discussed above the number of cases of abetment of suicide had remained constant as during 1997-2000 also only 15 cases were recorded.

During 1989-2000 (twelve years) total 31828 cases were recorded out of which 1228 cases were of women victimization which was 3.08% of the total cases. During 1989-92 total 8280 cases were recorded out of which 218 were the cases of women victimization which was 2.53% of the total cases during that period. Similarly during 1993-96, 10089 cases were reported out of which 392 were the cases of women victimization and thus amounted to 3.89% of the total number of crimes during this period showing an increase in percentage. Then during the period of 1997-2000, 13469 cases were recorded in total, of which 618 were the cases of crime against female section of society and this was 4.60% of the total cases reported during the period.

Summary and Conclusion

The present study includes the most commonly encountered

crimes against women during last 12 years (1989-2000) and these were as follows (increasing order).

Abetment of suicide (38)< chain snatching (96)< dowry deaths (101)< kidnapping and· abduction and assault or criminal force to woman to outrage her modesty (137 each)< rape (187)< eve teasing (251)< harassment for downy (291). During the period of 1989-92 cases of women victimization were 2-53% of total crimes, during 1993-96, this percentage was 3.89% and during 1997-2000 crimes against female members of society increased to 4.60% of the total number of crimes. Thus we can conclude that there is not only the gradual increase in number of cases of women victimization but the percentage of cases of women victimization of the total crimes is also increasing day-by-day.

5

Regression Analysis of Penetration Data on Window Pane and It's Impact Energy by Indian Made Soft Nose Bullet

*N.P. Waghmare**
*M.S. Rao***
*A.Manna****
*A.K. Pal**
*S.S. Badwal**

Abstract

In present paper, a statistical regression analysis of fracture, crater on window pane (glass sheets) by soft nose bullet made in kirkee Factory, India using a high velocity rifle having 6 land & 6 groove rifling has been done. Retardation laws of projectile, impulse transmitted on the glass target also have

* Central Forensic Science Laboratory, 30, Gorachand Road, Kolkata-700014.

** C.F.S., Directorate of Forensic Science, Govt. of India, New Delhi-110 003.

*** Prof. in Physics, Dept. of Physics, Jadavpur University, Kolkata.

been analysed. An experimental set up has been designed to investigate the projectile phenomena. A regression analysis of experimental data on windowpane correlated glass and its impact energy has been done for analysing the data and this data can be with the data obtained from the actual crime spot.

Different thickness of windowpane have been used to study the fracture of glass by said bullet.

Key words: Regression analysis, ammunition, firearm expert, glass pane, firearm, crime spot.

Introduction

Earlier workers observed, that the intermediate targets may influence the distribution of shots in the fatal wounds by shotgun, rifles and on the variety of objects like glass, door glass, windowpane screen. The other miscellaneous articles of target materials like cloths, may serve as intermediate targets for jacketed/non jacketed bullets, ricochet of bullets may become secondary projectile [1,2,3]. The methods are available for examination and comparison of glass fragments [4,5]. Past studies did not consider the loss of energy, impulse transmitted, pressure on impact, force of retardation on glass as intermediate target for the numerical regression analysis and its wounding behaviour on human being. Fracture characteristics of flat glass and its characteristics fracture marks formed on the crack surface under local as well as external stress conditions like high velocity projectile hitting the glass targets were studied [6,7,8].

Maheshwari, H.S. & Dhenge, S. had studied the regression analysis of size of window pane and its static pressure requirements for fracture [9]. Griffith (1920), Presten (1926), Haward (1944) and Anderson (1949) also showed that the variation in size of glass sheet may have a significant effect on its static pressure requirements for undergoing rupture. But abovementioned works were on phenomena of rupture of glass pane by keeping different pressure [10,11,12,13,].

Very little work is available on fracture and behaviour

of bullet on glass by high velocity projectiles, most of the authors worked on the fracture on glass by applying external pressure not by high velocity projectiles. Hence, we have taken the work on study of the behaviour of soft nose bullet on the window pan, which is easily and commercially available and normally used as window pane in house and offices, using the .315" sporting rifle made in Ordnance factory, India. These rifles are issued to people for sporting purpose and consequently it goes to hand in antisocial and criminals.

Methods and Materials:

In the present experimental study, we have used .315" calibre sporting rifle using soft pointed bullet fired through the commercial windowpane having the size 12 inch by 12 inch with different thickness i.e. 2.6mm, 3.8mm, 5.2mm and 8.2mm used for target material.

In this experiment two electronic timer made up of Electronic Corporation of India Limited were used to measure the striking and remaining velocity for different thickness of glass pane. The distance from the muzzle of the firearm to the front face of glass is changed. An attempt has been made to measure the impact of soft nose bullets were fired on different thickness of glass sheets held at right angle to the line of fire.

A regression analysis for the different thickness of glass sheets x and loss of impact/striking energy y required for fracture & perforation through the glass pane by soft nose bullet done in the present paper realizing the importance of result for the crime scene investigation. These results are shown in Table 1, 2 and 3.

Initially an attempt was made to establish a correlation between thickness of glass sheets and loss of energy which needed for fracture and loss during the travelling through the glass target.

Co-efficient of correlation (Kark Pearson 'r') between thickness of glasspane (x) caused to fracture by soft nose bullet and striking energy required to fracture, creator on the windowpane (y) can be calculated from the following formula:

$$r = \Sigma(x-x^{\cdot})\ (y-y^{\cdot})/\sqrt{\ \Sigma(x-x^{\cdot})^2\ \Sigma(y-y^{\cdot})^2}$$

where x is deviation from the thickness of glasspane (x) and y is the deviation from the mean loss of energy (y) respectively.

The coefficient of correlation between thickness of glass pane to loss of energy caused by the soft nose bullet and striking energy required to fracture and crater on window glass pane is determined.

It has been observed that the loss of energy, pressure on impact, retardation force on bullet and impulse transmitted increases with the thickness of glasspane. The variation depends upon the nature of ammunitions and other parameters like distance of firing, type and size of glass of the target and striking velocity. These results are shown in Figure 1,2,3 and 4.

Table 1 Data shows each fired bullets. All the bullets were unstable and tumbling on the emergence from the window pane.

(1) Nature of glass sheet: Plain, commercial and transparent windowpane.

(2) Number of observations: 12

(3) Firearms used for firing: Regular .315" caliber, made in ordinance factory, India.

(4) Ammunition used during the experimentation: .315"/8mm, K.F., 1993.

(5) Ballistic coefficient of projectile: 0.03353

(6) Weight of .315"/8mm projectile: 15.50 gm. (approx.)

No. of shots	Striking velocity for fracture glass ft/sec	Distance from muzzle to glass target. (inches)	Remaining velocity ft/sec.	Thickness of glass target (mm)	Size holes produced by bullet. (inches)	Retardation factor ft^{1} α
1.	1500	10.8	1123	2.6	0.475	0.2514
2.	1488	98	1120	2.6	0.775	0.2467
3.	1525	72	1210	2.6	0.711	0.2009
Mean						0.2327
4.	1620	72	1251	3.8	0.733	0.2245
5.	1605	120	1242	3.8	0.795	0.2227
6.	1540	120	1187	3.8	0.793	0.2261
Mean						0.2244
7.	1398	120	1000	5.2	0.702	0.2910
8.	1467	96	1093	5.2	0.815	0.2556
9.	1534	96	1150	5.2	0.581	0.2502
Mean						0.2656
10.	1745	96	1200	8.5	0.746	0.3252
11.	1576	96	1173	8.5	0.775	0.2565
12.	1642	96	1180	8.5	0.704	0.2869
Mean						0.2895

Table 3 Regression Data for loss of energy, impulse transmitted, pressure on impact and retadation force during the pssage of soft nose projectile through window pane.

Sl.No.	Thickness of window pane	Loss of energy ft.lbs	Impulse transmitted lb.s	Pressure on impact lb/in^2	Retardation force ft^1	Coefficient of correlation $R=\Sigma(x-\bar{x})(y-\bar{y})/\sqrt{\Sigma(x-\bar{x})^2\Sigma(y-\bar{y})^2}$
1.	2.6	513.03	0.3736	4695.08	0.2327	0.94166
2.	3.8	543.80	0.4031	5756.80	0.2244	1.137
3.	5.2	523.69	0.4627	5855.83	0.2656	0.000851
4.	8.5	714.86	0.4326	8233.37	0.2895	0.000740

Table 2
Numerical data on loss of velocity, energy and their percentage etc.

No. of shot	Loss of velocity ft/sec	Initial energy, ft.lbs.	Remaining energy, ft.lbs	Loss of velocity, %	Loss of energy,	Loss of energy, %	Impulse Transmitted I, lb. s	Pressure on impact P, lb/in^2
1	377	1240.0	673.35	25.13	566.67	37.77	0.4017	5819.44
2	368	1182.2	669.76	24.73	512.44	43.34	0.3921	5619.64
3	315	1241.7	781.72	20.65	460.00	37.04	0.3356	2404.10
Mean	*353*				*513.30*		*0.3736*	
4	369	1401.2	835.60	22.77	565.64	40.37	0.3932	6061.50
5	363	1375.4	823.62	22.61	551.80	40.13	0.3868	5902.00
6	353	1266.2	752.29	22.92	513.98	40.59	0.4241	5561.64
Mean	*361*				*543.80*		*0.4031*	
7	398	1043.5	533.93	28.46	509.58	48.85	0.3985	5851.11
8	374	1149.0	637.86	25.49	511.20	44.48	0.4091	5659.19
9	384	1256.4	706.12	25.03	550.30	43.79	0.5807	6057.19
Mean	*385*				*523.69*		*0.4627*	
10	545	1625.8	768.86	31.23	856.97	52.70	0.4294	10,187.6
11	403	1326.1	734.65	25.57	519.51	44.60	0.4923	6554.40
12	462	1429.5	743.44	28.13	696.12	48.37	0.3761	7958.12
Mean	*470*				*714.86*		*0.4326*	

Results and Discussions

In the present studies, .315"/8mm soft nose bullet fired through different thickness of glass were analyzed, initial velocity, remaining energy and impulse transmitted, pressure on impact and retardation force along with loss of velocity/loss of energy etc. were calculated and computed for correlating further case related data. Such behaviours of parameters have been studied in depth. For each single shot loss of velocity, remaining velocity, loss of energy, impulses transmitted were estimated. Their respective parameters analysis of regression calculations were also computed on the different thickness of glass.

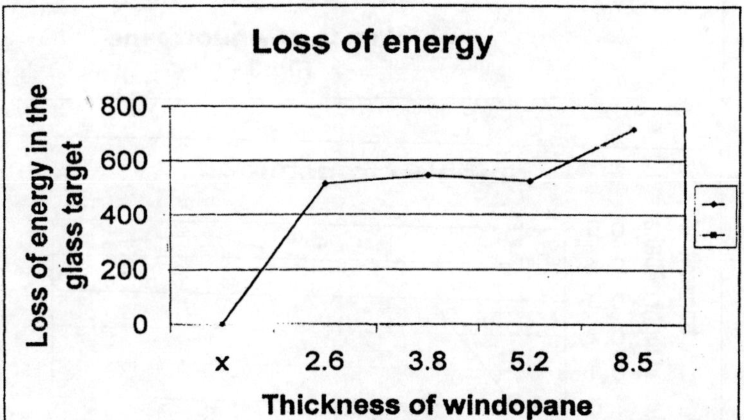

Fig.1

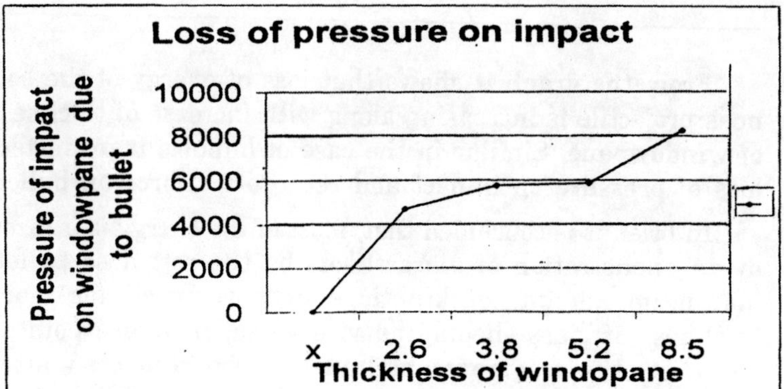

Fig.2

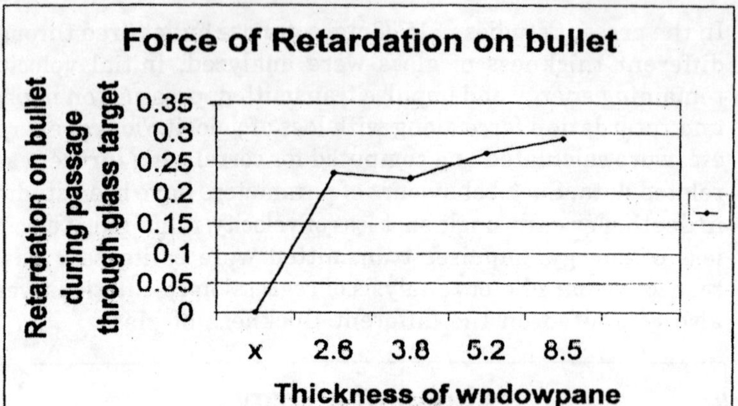

Fig.3

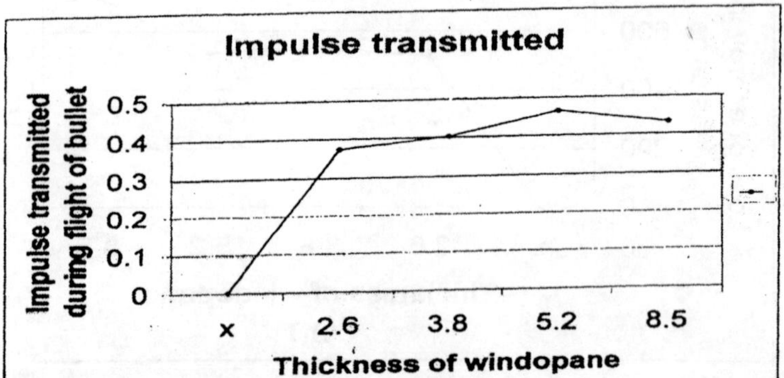

Fig.4

From the graph it shows that loss of energy of the soft noes projectile is increasing along with increase of thickness of windowpane. Similar in the case of impulse transmitted, loss of pressure on impact and retardation force on bullet.

In brief, it is concluded that, most of the energy is utilized during penetration of glass sheets by the soft nose bullet. Maximum amount of kinetic energy required for more thickness of glass sheets and vice versa. It is also pointed out that, the fragments of bullets were recovered after penetration of glass target with typical phenomena. The study of phenomena of bullet on the matrices used in forensic need is under progress with high-speed camera in the author's laboratory.

REFERENCES

1. Breitenecker. R. and Senior, W.J. Shotgun Patterns. I. An experimental study of the influence of intermediate targets, *Journals of Forensic Sciences,* Vol. 12, April, 1967. pp. 193-204.
2. DiMaio, V.J.M. and Spitz, W.U. 'Injury by birdshot", *Journal of Forensic Sciences,* Vol. 15, No. 3 July 1970, pp. 396-402.
3. Finck, P.A. 'Ballistics and pathologic aspects of missile wounds. Converstation between Anglo-American and metric-system units," *Military Medicine,* Vol. 130, No. 6, June 1965, pp. 545-569.
4. McLaughlin, G.H. and Beardsley, C.H., "Distance determinations in cases of gunshot through glass," *Journal of Forensic Science,* Vol. 1, No. 1, Jan. 1956, pp. 43-46.
5. *NRA Firearms and Ammunition Factbook,* National Rifle Association, Washington, D.C., 1964, p. 284.
6. Dowles R. and Sugarman B., "Glass Technology", 3, 156, (1962).
7. Marshall D.B., Lawn B.R. and Mecholsky J.J., *J. American Ceram. Soc.,* 57, 440 (1974).
8. Suzuki, J. and Shirahashi, J., *Proceedings of 1st International Conference on Mechanical Behaviour of Materials,* (Vol. 4, pp. 495, (1972).
9. Maheshwari H.S., Dhenge, S. "regression analysis plate", *J. Ind. Acad. of Forensic Sciences,* 28(2) 1989, 19.
10. Griffith., A.A., Phenomenon of rupture and flow in solids, *Trans. R. SOS,* 221, 163,1920.
11. Preston, F.W., A Study of rupture of glass, *J.Soc. Glass Tech.,* 10, 234, 1926.
12. Howard, R.N., "The behaviour of glass under impact and static loadign, *Jos. Glass Tech.,* 28, 1-32, 1944.
13. Anderson, O.L. "Griffith criteria foe factor, *Trans. Soc. Glass Tech,* 36,68.1949.

6

A Preliminary Report on Class Characteristics of Handwriting in School Children

*V. Roshan**
*B. Verma***
*N.K. Kanwal****
*P.K. Janjua*****

Abstract

The characteristics features of handwriting used for identification and comparison are mainly divided into two categories i.e. Class characteristics and Individual characteristics. In the present study class characteristics of handwriting in different school going children ranging in age 3-14 years were analyzed. A total of 200 samples (100 male, 100 female) from the area around Bundelkhand University, Jhansi (U.P.) were collected. The handwritings of these were carefully analyzed to study different class characteristics such as pen pressure, size, speed, spacing and tremors, hesitation

* Institute of Forensic Science & Criminology, B.U. Jhansi.

and pen pauses with the help of magnifying lenses. The observation shows considerable variations in the handwritings of different age group.

Introduction

The hand writing is certain visual signs or marks which are accepted by two or more fellowmen or group of person or individual of a town city or communication of informing one's ideas to other for a particular matter, or understanding or sending messages to other (Harrison, W.R.: *Suspect Documents & Their Scientific Examination).* Ames one stated that *"the peculiarity of style comes by evolution through times & circumstances."* The characteristic feature of handwriting used for identification comparison are mainly divided into two categories i.e. class characteristic and individual characteristic.

In the present study class characteristic of handwritings in different school going children ranging in age 3-14 years were analyzed. The handwriting of these was carefully analyzed. The handwriting of these was carcfully analyzed to study different class characteristic such as pen pressure, size, speed spacing hesitation tremor, and penpause with the help of magnifying glass.

Material & Methodology

Hand writing samples of 200 individuals (100 males, 100 females) were collected from the different schools near the vicinity of Bundelkhand University, Jhansi (U.P).

Some of the basic factors which were studied for analyzing these class characteristic were strokes, terminals indentations on paper, latter ends, pen lift, pen pauses tremors distance between letters lines & word, size of words these all characteristics were studied different magnifying lenses & other required instruments.

The above-mentioned studies were made in accordance to the process mentioned by following scientist *Osborn, A.S.:* Questioned Documents, 1929, *Harrison, W.R.:* Suspect Documents & Their Scientific Examination, 1960, *Hilton, O.:* The Scientific Examination of Questioned Document, *B.L.*

Saxena: Identification of Handwriting, Fingerprint, Footprint & Detection of Forgeries.

Results & Discussion

Age-Group	*No of Males*	*No. of Females*	*Total*
4-6	20	20	40
6-8	20	20	40
8-10	20	20	40
10-12	20	20	40
12-14	20	20	40
Total	100	100	200

A total of 200 samples were collected ranging from age group 4-14. In each group 40 samples were taken out of which 20 were males 720 were females. This was done to maintain the uniformity of data.

Ames once stated that "the *peculiarity of style comes by evolution through times & circumstances.*"

Pen Pressure

Age Group	*Graded*		*High*		*Normal*		*Low*	
	Male	*female*	*Male*	*female*	*Male*	*female*	*Male*	*female*
4-6	3	5	14	11	2	2	1	2
6-8	5	6	11	10	2	3	2	1
8-10	4	6	7	8	6	6	3	-
10-12	3	4	5	4	8	9	4	3
12-14	3	2	2	3	9	11	6	4

Heavy pen pressure was common in lower age group followed by graded pen pressure but in children of higher age group, Normal pen pressure was common followed by low pen pressure.

Size

Age-Group	*Small<5cm*		*Large size>5cm*		*Irregular*	
	Male	*female*	*Male*	*female*	*Male*	*female*
4-6	1	3	13	11	6	6
6-8	5	7	11	8	4	4
8-10	8	10	5	6	7	4
10-12	11	14	5	2	4	4
12-14	12	15	3	1	5	4

In lower age group, children, irregular and large size were more dominant but in children of higher age group the small size letter were more common.

Lower age group showed generally uneven spacing between letter, words and lines whereas higher age group children showed even spacing between lines letters and words.

Speed

Age Group	*Slow*		*Normal*		*Fast*	
	Male	*female*	*Male*	*female*	*Male*	*female*
4-6	12	13	6	4	2	3
6-8	12	11	5	6	3	3
8-10	7	6	8	10	5	4
10-12	4	3	10	9	6	8
12-14	2	1	8	7	10	12

Speed of the writing of children of lower age group was generally slow but with increase in age there was a considerable shift in handwriting speed from slow to high & normal.

Spacing

Age—Group	*Spacing between words*				*Spacing between words*				*Spacing between letters*			
	Even		*Uneven*		*Even*		*Uneven*		*Even*		*Uneven*	
	Male	*female*	*Male*	*female*	*Male*	*female*	*Male*	*female*	*Male*	*female*	*Male*	*female*
4-6	9	8	11	12	3	4	17	16	6	8	14	12
6-8	12	10	8	10	5	7	15	13	7	5	13	15
8-10	15	13	5	7	9	8	11	12	10	9	10	11
10-12	16	15	4	5	11	9	9	11	11	13	9	7
12-14	17	15	3	5	14	12	6	8	14	15	6	5

Tremor/Hesitation/Pen Pauses

Age Group	*Showed*		*Did not show*	
	Male	*female*	*Male*	*female*
4-6	19	18	1	2
6-8	16	13	4	7
8-10	8	9	12	11
10-12	4	5	16	15
12-14	1	2	19	18

Tremor, Hesitation and pen pauses were more in the lower age group children but it diminished considerably in higher age group children.

Summary

The observation shows considerable variation in the handwriting of different age groups. Children of lower age group showed inferior quality of handwriting but in children of higher age group quality of handwriting were quiet improved.

REFERENCES

1. Osborn, A.S.: *Questioned Documents,* 1929.
2. Harrison, W.R.: *Suspect Document and Their Scientific Examination,* 1960.
3. Hilton, O.: *The Scientific Examination of Questioned Document.*
4. B.L. Saxena: *Identification of Handwriting, Fingerprint, and Footprint & Detection of Forgeries.*
5. Ames: Ames on Forgery, 1900.

7

White Collar Crime – An Unperceived Area of Crime

*Pallavi Gupta**

Introduction

It is common knowledge that certain professions offer lucrative opportunities for criminal acts and unethical practices which hardly attract public attention. There have been crooks and unethical persons in business, various professions and even in public life. These deviants have scant regard for honesty and other ethical values. Therefore they carry on their illegal activities with impunity without the fear of loss of prestige or status. The crimes of this nature are called 'white collar crime' and they are essentially an outcome of competitive economy.

Historical Background

If we see the historical background of such type of crime in 1892 it was Prof. Edwin C. Hill, who read a paper titled 'criminal capitalists' before the International Congress on the Prevention and Repression of Crime at London. In this paper he underlined

* Lecturer, Institute of Law, Bundelkhand University, Jhansi.

the growing incidence of crime as an organised business and its evil effects on society. In 1934 Albert Morvis asserted that anti social activities of persons of high status committed in course of their profession must be brought within the category of crime should be made punishable.

Finally Prof. S.H. Sutherland emphasized that 'upper world' crimes committed by persons of upper socio-economic groups in course of their occupation violating the trust should be termed "white collar crime" which is different from blue collar crime (Traditional crime) for example. If a broker shoots his wife's lover, that is not a white collar crime, but if he violates the law and is convicted in connection with his business, he is a white collar criminal. Thus the distinction between white collar crime and blue collar crime could be based on the extent of presumed respectability. Thus if a person who belongs to a respectable class of society and possesses some degree of good reputation, sells shoddy goods, he is committing a white collar crime. But if a group of persons unknown to their victims, sell the same type of shoddy goods, that would not be a white collar crime.

Definition

Therefore for the first time white collar crime, defined by Prof. Sutherland as a crime committed by person of respectability and high social status in course of their occupation. A white collar criminal belong to upper socio-economic class who violates the criminal law while conducting his professional qualities.

Thus Sutherland's definition of white collar crime consists of four criteria, namely:

(1) a crime

(2) committed by a person of respectability and

(3) of high Social status

(4) in the course of his/her occupation.

But his definition was not proper it was criticized by many authors as white collar crime come within the preview of the special commissions, Tribunals and Boards instead of normal criminal justice administrator, therefore they can't result into conviction in real sense of the term. White collar crime includes even those violation of law which are not committed in course of occupation and these violations do not necessarily belong to upper strata of society or the so called prestigious group e.g.. Tax evasion, it is not committed in course of occupation and it can be committed by persons belongs to upper, middle or even lower strata of society. For a white collar crime mensrea is not necessarily required which is an essential ingredient of a crime.

Therefore "violation of trust" is included as a fifth element in the definition of white collar crime.

Sir Walter Reckless suggests that white collar crime represent the of offences of business man who are in a position to determine the policies and activities of business. Some authorities suggests that white collar crimes are committed by persons of status not for need but for greed.

As a consequences we see that while collar crime is more dangerous to society and financial loss to society from white collar crime is far greater than the financial loss from the blue collar crime. The most dismal aspect of white collar crime is that there is no effective program for the enforcement of criminal law against them and the influential persons involved in these crime are able to resist enforcement of law against themselves.

Nature

If we see the nature of white collar is that the injury caused by such crime is so widely diffused in the large body of society that their gravity in regard to individual victim is almost negligible. This is reason that these crimes did not attract much attention that they do not carry with them any loss of social status of the offender even if he is caught. Escaping prosecution is yet another reason for white collar criminals. In case of misrepresentation, concealment or fraud etc., the courts usually place reliance on the principle of caveat-emptor, which signifies that the purchaser must enter into a deal with open eyes and guard himself against ordinary dishonesty of the vendor.

You know as a result of this attitude of the court there was enormous increase in white collar crime during the period of depression in 1930's in United State. This is the reason that American president Rooswelt in 1933 insisted on withdrawal of the caveat-emptor from adjudication of cases involving white collar crime.

Barnes and Tealers quoted Lord Acton who said "power tends to corrupt and absolute power tends to corrupt absolutely." Whenever citizens of a particular community become apathetic to the working of their Govt., grafts, corruption and alliance between public servant and the criminal world are common phenomenon resulting into breach of trust, fraud and other malpractices. In 1992 the scam of Hurshad Metha is burning illustration due to which our country suffered financial crimes. In 1995 Telecom tender scam, 1996, Hawala scam, Bihar Fodder scam, before this Mundhra scam 1971, Antule scam, Churhut lauttary scam, latest Tahelka dot com, Jayalalita scam, proved that how politician and higher authorities and bureaucrats were involved in such type of white collar criminality.

No doubt white collar criminality thrives because of public apathy to it. The reason for this public insensibility is that firstly such criminal operate with in the strict letter of law and exploit the credibility of their victims, and second, the legal battles involved are dragged out for years in the courts, with the result the gravity of the offence is completely lost in the oblivion.

Another important point in context of white collar crime is the member of the community themselves contribute to the commission of various white collar crimes willingly or unwillingly. For instance, illegal gratification to public servants to get the work done quickly, back marketing in time of scarcity, evasive price violations, rent ceiling violation etc., are examples where 'victims' of the crime are themselves to be blamed for involvement in white collar criminality. In fact such crime can't be committed unless there is a demand for illegal favour from consumers and they are actively involved in the deal.

As per the 29th report of Law Commission the modern

scientific and technological development and monopolistic trends in business world have lead to enormous more ever it is very difficult to obtain statistics about some type of white collar crime.

Kinds of White Collar Crimes

Edel Rertz, classified white collar crimes in the following three categories:

1. Personal crimes—Crime by persons operating on an individual for personal gains in a non business context.
2. Abuses of trust—Occupational crimes in violating the duty of loyalty and fidelity to the employer or client.
3. Business crimes—Crimes incidentals to and in furtherance of business operations.

White Collar Crimes in India

1. In Trade and Industry.
2. Hording, profiteering and black marketing of essential commodities.
3. Violation of Foreign Exchange Regulations and Import and Export Act.
4. Adulteration.
5. Violation of Tax Laws.
6. Corruption in Government, and politics.
7. White collar crimes in professions;
   - Medical profession,
   - Legal profession,
   - Engineering,
   - Educational Institution.
8. Black money, dirty money and money laundering techniques.

Business, Trade, Commerce and Industry

Prof. Sutherland emphasized the high degree of criminality to business world which includes traders, businessmen and industrialist. They are involved in illegal contracts combintations or conspiracies in restraint of trade, misrepresentation in advertising infringements against copyrights and trade marks, unfair labour practices, bribing public officials and so on. The public hardly knows the trickery of business criminals as they trade it is not so important for their purpose. The Santhanam Committee gave a graphic account of misdeeds of businessmen in the following words "corruption can exists only if there is someone willing to corrupt and capable of corrupting. This willingness and capacity to corrupt is found in a large measure in the industrial and commercial classes."

Two instances of big business criminality are provided by reports made by the Vivian Bose Commission dealing with the notorious Dalmia-Jain and Mundhra cases. This commission held them responsible in different degrees for fraud, mismanagement, manipulation of accounts, destruction of records, personal gain at the expenses of the investing public, avoidance of taxes and a number of irregularities and violation of trust.

Hoarding, Profiteering and Black Marketing of Essential Commodities

Hoarding and Black marketing of essential commodities by traders in India has become a chronic problem. Such traders are heartless antisocial criminals who deserve stringent penal action. Violation of foreign exchange regulations and Import and Export laws are frequently resorted to for the sake of huge profits. This is more prevalent among business and thereby denuding the National economy.

Adulteration

Adulteration of food stuffs, edibles and drug which causes irreparable danger to public health is another white collar crime, common in India. In India the problem is so wide spread that from 25% to 75% of most of the food stuffs consumed in this country are adulterated. The same is true of the production of spurious drugs in the country. It is due to the artificial scarcity created by manufacturers and also due to the ignorance and poverty of the consumers who go in for cheap medicine.

Violation of Taxation Laws

Frequent Tax violation which occur in India are in the area of Income tax, Wealth tax, Estate duty and Sales tax. The loss resulting from the violations to the state exchequer is tremendous. It is undoubted fact that the actual Tax paid is only a fraction of the total income and rest goes as black money. The white collar criminals succeeded in accumulating the 'black money' in converting into 'white money' by various methods. This menace has serious repercussion in the economy of the country.

Corruption in Government and Politics

Corruption in Government and Politics is a global phenomenon. Corruption in its modern and wider sense, include all forms of dishonest gains in case, kind or position by person in Government. Two Government departments which have been traditionally notorious for corruption in the country are those of Police and public works. The political corruption includes the grafts, abuse of good offices, violation of election Laws etc.

White collar crime in Profession

Some of the professions involving technical expertise and skill provide sufficient opportunities for white collar criminality. They include medical profession, engineering, legal practice, private educational institutions etc.

Medical Profession

Issue of false medical certificates, purposely prolonging the treatment with ulterior motivates for money, illegal abortions, secret services to criminals for their aquittal, doctors. Practicing as expert and administering medicines and injection without knowing the repercussions on the life of the patients are some of the white collar crimes committed by them.

The usual legal professional violations committed by lawyer are—aiding and advising organized gang criminals, preparing false and fabricated claims and fabricating evidences, delaying the litigation by colluding with the opposite party, and adopting unscrupulous tactics, violating all ethnical norms of the legal profession are some of these types.

Engineering—the evidence of white collar crime is fairly high among some other professionals also like advertisers, property valuers, consulting and other engineers and other kind of work.

Educational Institution

The worst affected are the private educational institutions which are run with the girl and they normally make and fake and bogus enrolment of students meagre salary to teacher while getting the signature for full salary, fraduing the large sums of Government grants, issue of fictitious, bogus and manipulative certificates, collection of unauthorized donations are some the white collar crime. Insurance of fake degree and diplomas by the unrecognized institutions is also more prevalent.

With the increasing use of newly developed technologies in the various spheres (of business, commerce and industry) particularly the computers, the scope of w.c.c. is getting wide, new crimes are emerging and the commission of certain kinds of pre-existing. Crime is being greatly facilitated.

White collar crime has to be placed on the same footing as "mass disobedience" of laws in a public opinion, which looks upon absolute business practice as necessary for successful performance even if they are illegal. The result is "mass neutralization of law and order which gives rise to a group norm which approves w.c.c. as a normal response particularly when the social and power status of the offender gives him a distinct advantage in the practical operating of the law."

The quantification of white collar crime in a pluralistic society is not an easy task as its pervasiveness is deep-rooted and liberate in the socio-economic echelons under the banner of respectability and therefore white collar crime are also termed as hidden criminality.

Therefore it is not easy to assess the true extent of white collar criminality in a community, some of the reasons like complexity and impersonality of the offence and frequent lack of prosecution and punishment for white collar crime more ever the usual information on the extent of white collar crime. Crime in India magazine compiled by Bureau of Police Research and Development, ministry of Home Affairs hardly given my information of Govt. of India and the finding of the various tribunals and commission dealing with white collar crimes are possible sources.

Statistics regarding white collar crime are given by CRIME IN INDIA-1996 during 1991 to 1996 is as follows:

White Collar Crime

1991	1993	1995	1996
2.9	3.1	3.3	3.6

This data shows that white collar crimes have recorded only a marginal increase of nearly half% during 1993-1996.

Remedial Measures

In a country like India where large scale starvation, mass illiteracy, and ignorance affect the life of he people. Control of these crimes is a crucial problem for the criminal justice administration in this country. However some of the remedial measures for combating white collar criminality may be stated as follows—

- Creating public awareness against these through the media of press, platform and other audio-visual aids.
- Stringent regularity laws and drastic punishment for white collar criminals may have in reducing these crime. White collar criminals should be dealt sternly

by prescribing stiffer punishment keeping in view the gravity of injury caused to society because of these crimes. In this context the supreme court observed in M.H. Hoskot Vs. state of Maharashtra "Soft sentencing justice is gross injustice where many innocent are the potential victims.

- A separate chapter on white collar crime should incorporated in the Indian Penal Code by amending the code so that white collar criminals who are convicted by the court, do not escape punishment because of their high social status.
- There is an urgent need for a National Crime Commission which may squarely tackle the problem of crime and criminality in all its facts.
- Above all public vigilance seems to be the corner stone of anti collar crime strategy.
- As per the role of forensic science it should be developed in such a manner to investigate the cases of white collar crimes.

Role of Forensic Science

Forensic Science means application of science to law. This science applies scientific principles and method for the investigation of crime. A forensic science is essentially concerned with determination of identify as well as degree of individuality of tangible physical object associated with crime. Such information may have to be obtained from a speak, dirt metal, scrapping, bone pieces, chips of wood, prints fibres, hair tool marks, finger print, broken glass, explosive residues, biological stains and most of other physical material evidences, scientific date and expert opinion by the forensic scientist provides valuable links in the chain of even concerning a crime.

Here as data shows (given in table) that White Collar Crimes are increasing day by day like a slow poison, even area of White Collar Crime is also expanding, my suggestion to control the White Collar Crime are as following—

- Forensic Science should be developed in such a manner that White Collar Criminals could be traced out easily.
- No case concerning White Collar Crime should decide without taking the forensic science experts opinion. A tribunals must be constituted with forensic science expert.
- As we know forensic science laboratories are multi disciplinary institutions doing highly specialist analytical work all over the country, these laboratories should be established in every district to assists the court of law by primary report.

At last, being a law lecturer, my humble suggestion is that importance of forensic science is increasing day by day so forensic science as a compulsory paper should be inserted at L.L.B. level.

8

Reconstruction of Stature from Upper Extremity Bone Lengths

*Surinder Nath**

Introduction

Forensic Anthropologists apply standard scientific techniques developed in physical anthropology to the identification of skeletal remains badly decomposed or otherwise unidentified human remains. During examination of skeletal remains thcy attempt to determine origin, age, sex number of individuals involved and race besides determination of ante mortem height of the deceased. Out of all these aspects, determination of ante mortem height has attracted attention of most of researchers the world over. As a consequence of this different researchers have worked on various skeletal as well as living population groups and formulated means of stature reconstruction.

Thomas Dwight (1894) suggested two methods for reconstruction of stature from skeletal remains, i.e. Anatomical and Mathematical. The anatomical method involves in simply arranging the bones together, in

* Department of Anthropology, University of Delhi, Delhi- 110 007.

reproducing the curves of the spine, in making respective allowance for the soft parts and measuring the total length. This method is workable when a complete skeleton is available for examination. The mathematical method, on the other hand, is based on the relationship of individual long bone to the height of an individual and is workable even if a single long bone is available for examination. This method may be used either by computing Multiplication Factors (M.F.) or by formulating regression formulae, using a single bone for a combination of different long bone.

Due to the obvious disadvantage of using anatomical method where complete skeleton is required, Fully (1956) implemented certain modifications for its easy workability. He computed percentage contribution of each vertebra to the total height of the column. Thus using these values for missing vertebra and measuring the remaining, the height of the vertebral column is derived by a simple proportionality equation. Besides this Fully incorporated following cranial and postcranial measurements for the purpose of stature estimation:

1. Basion—bregma height,
2. First sacral segment height,
3. Oblique length of femur,
4. Tibial length, and
5. Tarsal height.

After obtaining these measurements and adding the total height of the vertebral column one may contain skeletal height, which can be used in the following regression equation to obtain living stature or ante mortem height.

Living stature=0.98 (total skeletal height) 14.63±2.05 cm

Fully further suggested addition of a correction factor (CF) to the stature thus obtained:

Estimated stature up to 153.5 cm add 10 cm to the result,

Estimated stature between 153.6 and 165.4 cm add 10.5 cm to the result,

Estimated stature above 165.5 cm adds 11.5 cm to the result.

The main advantage of Fully's method over the Dwight's is that one need not articulate the complete skeleton as described by Dwight. Secondly, this method is applicable universally to males and females of any population around the world.

Despite Fully's (1956) attempt to make the anatomical method workable even if a couple of vertebrae are missing as well as highlighting its universal applicability and greater accuracy in the predicted stature, the mathematical method gained more popularity with its obvious advantage that it is more convenient in use as it requires only length of the recovered long bone. The bone length may be entered into respective regression formulae or multiplied with the specific multiplication factor (M.F.) to obtain the estimated height. Somehow this method was in use even before Dwight could name it. Beddoes (1887) made the first attempt to estimate stature from femoral length of 'Older Races of England' for either sex. Subscquently Rollet (1888) published the earliest formal tables for determining statue using all the six long bones of the upper and the lower limbs of 50 male and 50 female French cadavers ranging in age from 24 to 99 years.

Manouvrier (1892) re-examined Rollet's data by excluding 26 males and 25 females above the age of 60 years and based his prediction tables on 24 males and 25 females. He suggested that the length of trunk declines by about 3 cm of their maximum stature due the effect of old age. The major difference between the approaches of Rollet and Manouvrier is that the latter determined the average stature of individuals who possessed the same length of a given long bone while the former determined and average length of a given long bone from individuals with identical stature. Manouvrier further suggested that while determining the stature from dried bones, 2 mm to be added to the bone length for cartilage loss and subsequently 2 cm should be added to the corresponding stature to convert the cadaver stature to the living stature.

Pearson (1899), using Rollet's data developed regression

equations for prediction of stature from long bone lengths. He restricted his study to four bones only, i.e. humerus, radius, femur and tibia. His approach to stature estimation was based on regression theory, which involves the calculation of standard deviations for the series of long bones and of coefficients of correlations between the different bone lengths and stature. Pearson's study not only changed the prevailing approach to the stature estimation by providing a more truly "mathematical method" but he departed in other ways from previous practices.

Stevenson (1929) computed regression formulae for Chinese and compared them with the Pearson's formulae. He observed that there is statistical improbability of the order of several millions to one that the formulae of one race would provide a satisfactory prediction of stature of an individual belonging to another group.

Subsequently several researchers formulated population and sex specific regression formulae using all the six long bones belonging to the upper and the lower limbs (Mendes Correa, 1932; Breitinger, 1937; Tellka, 1950; Dupertuis and Hadden, 1951; Trotter and Gleser, 1952; 1958; Fuji, 1958; Wells, 1959; Genoves, 1967; Kolte and Bansal, 1974; Oliver et al 1978; Yung-Hao et al, 1979; Cerny and Komenda, 1982; Shitai, 1983; Lundy, 1983; Boldson, 1984; Badkur; 1985; Kodagoda and Jayasinghe, 1988).

The alternative mathematical approach of stature estimation; i.e. the use of Multiplication Factor (MF),. was first advocated by Pan (1924) who formulated MFs for all the six long bones by simply computing the proportion of the said bone to the stature.

Multiplication Factor (MF) = Stature/Bone length

The average MF could be used to estimate the stature.

Subsequently this approach was adopted by various researchers (Nat, 1931; Siddique and Shah, 1944; Singh and Sohal, 1952; Kata and Majumadar, 1976; Badkur, 1985; Banerjee et al. 1944) on different Indian skeletal populations. Like the regression formulae, these MFs are also population and sex specific and should not be used interchangeably (Nath, 1996).

In connection with the use of regression formulae and MFs for estimation of stature Eliakis et al. (1966) are of the opinion that it is necessary to make regression equations or prediction tables for every race and its sub races. While Meadows and Janta (1995) observed that secular increase in the lower limb bone length is accompanied by relatively longer tibiae and suggested that the secular changes in proportion should be considered while formulating regression formulae for reconstruction of stature.

Out of the two methods of stature reconstruction, it is observed that the mathematical one is based on the relative proportion of bone lengths to height but it does not take into account the varying proportions of trunk length to total stature. The anatomical method, on the other hand, by including spine length when measuring skeletal height addresses this source of variation and thus provides greater accuracy in the estimated height.

Secondly the correction factor, which is added to the skeletal height while using anatomical method, compensates for the thickness of the soft tissues at the scalp, soles and cartilages of the joints. There is no evidence that these soft tissues differ from one population to another and thus we get a single equation irrespective of sexes for all the population groups.

The anatomical method also provides a possibility to regress individual long bones against skeletal samples lacking living stature or cadaver lengths. These equations only require addition of Fully's correction factor for the soft tissues to obtain estimated stature. One major drawback of this method is that it requires nearly complete skeleton for its implementation. Thus the first choice of the investigator is to employ the modified anatomical method provided that the skeleton is sufficiently complete. But in its absence one has to rely on the mathematical method.

In the present study an attempt has been made to formulate sex specific regression equations for estimation of stature using all the three long bones of the upper limb.

Material and Methods

To accomplish the aims of the present study all the three long bones, i.e. humerus, radius, and ulna, belonging to the right and the left sides of 82 male and 62 female skeletons were measured. This provided a total of 864 bones (492 male and 372 female). Each bone was measured for maximum length in accordance with the standard technique (Martin and Saller, 1959) and the documented stature was recorded for all the 144 skeletons (82 male and 62 female).

Data were subjected to statistical analysis for assessing bilateral and sex differences in the length of all the bones as well as stature. Bone lengths were subsequently correlated with the stature for formulation of sex specific regression equations for estimation of stature from these long bones.

Results

Table 1 presents and mean values and standard deviation for the right and the left side bones of male and female skeletons to observe the bilateral variations, if any. It is evident from the table that all the bones of the right side are longer than the left ones for both the sexes. The apparent variations observed in the length of these long bones reveal non-significant bilateral differences for both the sexes. Thus the sides (right and left) have been pooled to assess the sex differences.

Table 2 exhibits the mean values and standard deviation for the pooled (right and left) maximum lengths of humerus, radius and ulna of male and female skeletons. It is clear from the table that the male bones are sufficiently longer than the female ones and the sex differences, as assessed through t- test are highly significant ($p<0.001$) for all the three bones of the upper extremity as well as for stature.

Table 3 lists the values of correlation constant between stature and all the three long bones for males along with the respective regression equations for reconstruction of stature. The formulae for estimation of stature are listed in order of their standard error of estimate (SEE), from the smallest to the largest. It is observed that humerus exhibits the highest correlation with stature followed by ulna and radius.

Table 4 presents the values of correlation coefficient between stature and the three bone lengths of the upper extremity among females along with the linear regression equations for estimation of stature. These equations are listed in order of their SEE, from the smallest to the largest. It is evident that the humerus exhibits the highest correlation with stature followed by radius and ulna.

A careful examination of tables 3 and 4 reveal that the female bones not only show higher correlation with stature than the males but they also exhibit relatively low standard error of estimate indicating that the estimated stature using female bones would be more reliable than the ones obtained using male bones. It is also clear that humerus, as it exhibits the least SEE and the highest correlation with stature would provide the most reliable estimate of stature for both males and females.

Discussion

Pearson (1899) remarked that the extension of the regression formulae from one local race to another must be made with great caution. Stevenson (1929), one the other hand, actually demonstrated this by using Pearson's formulae on Chinese data and observed that there exists a statistical improbability of the order of several million to one that the formulae of one race would yield satisfactory prediction of stature of an individual belonging to another racial group. Subsequently, Lundy (1983) used the regression equations formulated by Trotter and Gleser (1952) on American Negro males to determine the stature of South African Negro males, using the mean long bone lengths of South African Negro males. He observed that in all cases the estimated stature using Trotter and Gleser's formulae are greater than the one obtained using equations derived from South African Negro samples. It was observed the equations derived from South African Negro data provide less variation in estimated stature for different long bones than do the American formulae.

In the present study a similar attempt has been made to predict stature of Indian male and female skeletal material using regression formulae formulated on American White males (Trotter and Gleser, 1959) and females (Trotter and Gleser, 1952), European Males and females (Oliver et.al., 1978), South African males and females (Lundy and Fieldsman, 1987), Mongoloid males (Trotter and Gleser, 1958) and Chinese males (Xiang-Quing, 1989) for humerus, radius and ulna bones of the upper limb. For estimation of stature the mean bone lengths of humerus, radius and ulna of the present study (Table 2) were used in different prediction formulae and the estimated stature and its difference from the actual stature for males and females is presented in Table 5.

It is evident from table 5 that the predicted stature for males using humerus is greater than the actual stature on using regression formulae for American whites, South Africans and Mongoloids while for the remaining groups the predicted stature is less than the actual one. The overall variation is observed to be between -2.4 cm among European males and +8.45 cm among South African males. While among females all the groups exhibit greater estimated stature than the actual one except for South Africans. The overall range being -9.70 cm among South Africans and +4.44 cm among American Whites.

In contrast to the predicted stature using humerus, radius exhibits a vide variation as among males the predicted stature is greater for all the groups except for South Africans. The overall range being-15.54 cm among South Africans to +15.52 cm among Afro-Americans. Whereas in case of females the variation is much greater than the one observed in case of humerus but it is relatively less than the one observed among males. It is observed that out of the three groups under comparison two exhibit greater estimated stature than the actual one and the estimated values fluctuate between— 10.02 cm among South Africans and +11.31 cm among American Whites.

Estimated stature using ulna also exhibits relatively greater variation than the one observed on using humerus.

Among males all the groups exhibit greater predicted stature except for South Africans and the values range from -15.03 cm among South Africans to +8.97 cm among American Whites. In case of famales the situation is more or less identical as only South Africans exhibit low estimates of staute and the estimated stature ranges between a minimum of -12.50 cm among South Africans and a maximum of +12.52 cm among Europeans.

On using the regression equations formulated in the present study yield the estimated stature in the range of—0.17 cm with humerus to +0.14 with ulna among males while in case of females the range is between -.0.09 cm with ulna and -0.16 cm with humerus. This clearly indicates that the regression formulae are both population specific and should not be extended on other population groups belonging to any part of the world.

Table 1
Bilateral Differences in Different bone Lengths

Bone	*Sex*	*Right*		*Left*		*Value of*
		Mean (mm)	*S.D*	*Mean (mm)*	*S.D*	*t*
Hum	Male	313.8	11.3	312.8	16.4	0.401
	Female	301.8	17.9	299.9	17.3	0.601
Rad	Male	246.5	12.1	244.3	12.6	1.122
	Female	234.2	13.0	232.8	13.5	0.592
Ulna	Male	265.6	13.2	263.7	13.8	0.889
	Female	252.4	13.4	251.4	13.4	0.428

Table 2
Sex Differences in Bone Lengths of the Upper Extremity and Stature

Bone Length/Stature	*Male*		*Female*		*Value of t*
	Mean (mm)	*S.D*	*Mean (mm)*	*S.D.*	
Humerus	312.7	16.4	299.9	17.3	4.526*
Radius	245.5	12.4	233.5	13.3	7.813*
Ulna	264.7	13.6	251.9	13.4	7.936*
Stature	1661.1	35.5	1542.9	40.2	26.516

* Significant at 0.01% level (p<0.001)

Table 3
Regression Equations for Estimation of Stature through Upper Extremity Bone Lengths among Males

Regression Equations	*See*	*Value of r*
S = 1209.2+1.44 (Humerus)	27.38	0.655
S = 1305.2 + 1.45 (Radius)	30.42	0.501
S = 1294.6 + 1.39 (Ulna)	30.91	0.522

Table 4
Regression Equations for Estimation of Stature through Upper Extremity Bone Lengths among Females

Regression Equations	*See*	*Value of r*
S = 1010.5 + 1.77 (Humerus)	25.58	0.776
S = 1023.3 + 2.22 (Radius)	27.36	0.738
S = 1003.1 + 2.14 (Ulna)	28.28	0.715

REFERENCES

Badkur, P. Estimation of bone length and stature from measurements of human long bones of Madhya Pradesh, India. Unpublished PhD thesis. University of Delhi, Delhi, (1985).

Banerjec, P.K, Mandi, A and Majumdar, M. Linear Correlation of different bones and stature—A study an Indian skeletons. *J. Ind. Acad. For SCi.* 33:13-18(1994).

Beddoe, J., On the stature of the older races of England, as estimated from the long bones. *JRAI.* 17: 202-207, (1887).

Boldsen. J., A statistical evaluation of the basis for predicting stature from the lenghts of the long bones in European populatins. *Am. J. Phys. Anthrop.* 65:301-311, (1984).

Breitinger, E., Zur berechnung der korperhuhe aus den langen glieidmassenknochen. *Anthrop. Anz:* 14:249-274, (1937).

Cerny, M. and St. Komenda. Reconstruction of body height based on humeus and femur lengths. Second Anthropological Congress of A.Hardlicka—Universitas Carolina, *Pragensis:* 475-479, (1982).

Dupertis, C.W. and Hadden, J.A., On the reconstruction of stature from the logn bones. *Am. J. Phys. Anthrop.* 9:15:53, (1951).

Dwight, T., Methods of estimating stature from parts of the skeleton. *Med. Rec. N.Y.* 46: 293-296, (1984).

Eliakis, C.E. Eliakis, and P. Iordanidid. Determination de la taille d'apres la mesuration des os longs. *Ann. Med. Leg* 46: 403-421, (1966).

Fujii, A. On the relation of long bone length of limbs to stature. *Juntendo Daigaku Taiiku Gakubu Kiyo,* 3:44-91, (1958).

Fully, G.M. Uno nouvelle methode de determination de le taille. *Ann. Med.Leg.* 35:266-273, (1956).

Genoves, S. Proportionality of the long bones and their relation to stature among Mesoamericans. *am. J.Phys. Anthrop,* 26:67-78, (1967)..

Kodagoda, A and Jayasinghe, S. A preliminary test of Pearson's formula for the estimation of height of the Sri Lankans. *For. Sci. Int,* 36:241-246, (1988).

Kolte, P.M. and Bansal, P.C. Determination of regression formulae for reconstructio of stature from the long bones of upper limbs in Maharashtrians of marathwada region. *J. Anat. Soc. Ind,* 23:1-11, (1974).

Lundy, J.K., Regression Equations for estimating living stature from long limb bones in the South African Negro. *South African Journal of Science.*79:337-338, (1983).

Lundy, J.K. and Feldesman, M.R. Revised equations for estimating living stature from the long bones of the South African negro. *South African Journal of Science.* 83:54-55, (1987).

Monouvrier, L. Determination de la taille d'apres les grands os des membres. *Rev. Mem. de L'Ecole D'Anth.*2:227-233, (1892).

Martin, R. and Saller, K. *Lehrbuch der Anthropologie in systematicher.* Fisher Darstellung, Stuttgart (1959).

Medows, L. and Jants, R.L. Allometric secular change in the long bones from 1800s to the present. *J. For. Sci.,* 40:762-767, (1995).

Mendes-Correa, A.A., La taille des Portugais d'apres les os longes. *Anthropologie,* Prague. 10;268-272, (1932).

Nat, B.S., Estimation of stature from long bones of the United Provinces: A mediço-legal inquiry in Anthropometry. *Ind. Med. Res.* 18:1245-1253, (1931).

Nath, S., *Forensic Anthropology,* Ashtam Prakashan, Delhi, (1996).

Oliver, G. Aaron, C. Fully, G and Tissier, G. New estimations of stature and cranial capacity in modern man. *J. Hum. Evol.,* 7:513-518, (1978).

Pan, N. Length of long bones and their proportion to body height in Hindus. *Anat,* 58:374-378, (1924.

Pearson, K. Mathematical contribution to the theory of evolution on reconstruction of stature of prehistoric races. *Phil. Trans. R. Soc. Lond. Series. A.* 192: 169-244, (1899).

Rollet, E. *De la mensurtion de os long des members dans ses rapports avec l'anthropologie la clinique et la medecine judicaire.* Lyon (1888).

Sthai, M.O., Estimation of Stature by long bones of Chinese male adults in south China. *Acta Anthrop. Sin.* 2:80-85, (1983).

Siddiqui, M.A.H. and Shah, M.A., Estimation of stature from long bons of Punjabis. *Ind. J. Med. Res.* 32: 105-108, (1944).

Singh, B. and Sohal, H.S. Estimation of stature from the length of clavicle in Punjabees: A preliminary report, *Ind. J. Med. Res.* 40:67-71, (1952).

Stevenson, P.H. On racial differences in stature long bone regression formulae with special reference to statur reconstruction formulae for Chinese. *Biom.* 21:303-318, (1928).

Telkka, A. On the prediction of human stature from the long Bones. *Acta Anat.* 9: 103-117, (1950).

Trotter, M. and Gleser, G.C. A re-evaluation of estimation of stature based on measurements of stature taken during life and of long bones after death. *Am. J. Phys. Anthrop.* 16:P69-123, 91958).

Wells, L.H. Estimation of stature from long bones: A reassessment *J. For. Med.* 6: 171-177, (1959).

Yung-hao, W, Chila-Ying and H.Ping-Cheng. Estimation of stature from logn bones of chinese male adults in southwest district. *Acta Anat. Sin* 10:1-6, (1979).

Table 5

Difference observed in Estimated Stature on using Lengths of HUMERUS, RADIUS and ULNA of the present study (Males-Humeral Length=31.27 cm; Radial Length=24.54 cm; Ulnar Length=26.47 cm; Females-Humeral Lengtth=29.99 cm; Radial; Length=23.35; Ulnar length=25.19 cm) in Regression Equations formulated for Different Populations of the World

S.No.	*Regression Equations*	*Actual Stature*	*Estimated Stature*	*Difference*	*Authors/ Year*	*Population/Sex*
1.	2.89 HUM +78.10	166.10	168.47	+2.37	Trotter & Gleser, 1958	American White, Males
2.	3.79 RAD+79.42	166.10	172.42	+6.32	-do-	-do-
3.	3.76 ULNA+75.55	166.10	175.07	+8.97	-do-	-do-
4.	3.36HUM+57.97	154.29	158.73	+4.44	Trotter & Gleser, 1952	American White, Females
5.	4.74RAD+54.93	154.29	165.60	+11.31	-do-	-do-
6.	4.27ULNA+57.76	154.29	165.23	+11.03	-do-	-do-
7.	3.19HUM+64.19	166.10	163.96	-2.14	Oliver et al. 1978	European Males
8.	3.96ULNA+66.71	166.10	171.48	+5.38	-do-	-do-
9.	3.09HUM+62.31	154.29	154.92	+0.63	Oliver et al. 1987	European Females
10.	4.09ULNA+63.71	154.29	166.81	=12.53	-do-	-do-

Table 5 (Contd.)

S.No.	*Regression Equations*	*Actual Stature*	*Estimated Stature*	*Difference*	*Authors/ Year*	*Population/Sex*
11.	2.88HUM+75.48	166.10	165.53	-0.57	Trotter & Gleser, 1958	Afro-American Males
12.	3.92RAD+85.43	166.10	181.62	+15.52	-do-	-do-
13.	3.20ULNA+82.77	166.10	167.47	+1.37	-do-	-do-
14.	3.08HUM+64.67	154.29	157.03	_2.74	Trotter & Gleser, 1952	Afro-American Females
15.	3.67RAD+71.79	154.29	157.48	+2.19	-do-	-do-
16.	3.20ULNA+75.38	154.29	158.75	+4.46	-do-	-do-
17.	2.89HUM+60.21	166.10	174.55	+8.45	Lundy & Feldesman, 1987	South African Males
18.	3.19RAD+72.14	166.10	150.56	-15.54	-do-	-do-
19.	2.96ULNA+7270	166.10	151.07	-15.03	-do-	-do-
20.	3.29HUM+45.89	154.29	144.59	-9.70	Lundy & Feldesman, 1987	South African Females
21.	4.16RAD+47.12	154.29	144.27	-10.02	-do-	-do-
22.	3.82.ULNA+47.57	154.29	141.79	-12.50	-do-	-do-
23.	2.68HUM+83.19	166.10	166.99	+0.89	Trotter & Gleser, 1958	Mongoloid Males
24.	3.54RAD+82.00	166.10	168.87	+2.77	-do-	-do-

25.	3.48ULNA+77.45	166.10	169.56	+3.46	-do-	-do-
26.	2.66HUM+82.64	166.10	165.81	-0.29	Xiang-Qing, 1989	Chinese Males
27.	349RAD+82.71	166.10	168.35	-2.25	-do-	-do-
28.	2.86ULNA+92.82	166.10	168.52	+2.42	-do-	-do-
29.	1.44HUM+210.91	166.10	165.93	-0.17	Present Study	Indian Males
30.	1.45RAD+130.51	166.10	166.09	-0.01	-do-	-do-
31.	1.39ULNA+129.45	166.10	166.24	+0.14	-do-	-do-
32.	1.77HUM+101.05	154.29	154.13	-0.16	-do-	Indian Females
33.	2.22RAD+102.33	154.029	154.16	-0.13	-do-	-do-
34.	2.14ULNA+100.30	154.29	154.20	-0.09	-do-	-do-

Hum =Humerus; Rad=Radius;

Range of Variation in Estimated Stature on using Different Regression Equations

Males:

Humerus: -2.14 cm to + 8.45 cm,

Radius: -15.54 cm to + 15.52 cm,

Ulna: -15.03 cm to + 8.97 cm,

FEMALES:

Humerus: -9.70 cm to + 4.44 cm,

Radius: -10.02 cm to + 11.31 cm,

Ulna: -12.50 cm to + 12.52 cm.

9

Study of Physical Dependence of Chronic Pentazocine Administered Albino Rats

*M.I. Shah**

*H.S. Maheshwari***

*S.K. Jain****

Abstract

Pentazocine is abused due to its psychotomimetic effects such as uncontrollable though, anxiety, nightmares, hallucination and euphoria. It is an important synthetic opioid analgesic drug of benzomorphan derivative compound.

The paper deals with physical dependence (degree illness) of albino rat after discontinuation of pentazocine from its chronic administration. Seven groups of albino rats each comprising of five animals were chosen. Group one was kept as control and remaining groups were exposed to pentazocine with daily does of 0.05 mg 100 gm^{-1} (+ ED_{50}) up to 30, 60, 90, 120, 150 and 180 days respectively. After completion of

*, **, ***, Department of Criminology and Forensic Science, Sagar University, Sagar, (Madhya Pradesh).

above periods the drug administration was suspended and daily observation of loss of body weight, elevation of body temperature, lachrymation and rhinorrhoae was noticed for the next week.

It has been observed that, no significant physical dependence was found in the matter of loss of body weight, elevation of body temperature, indiced of lachrymation and rhinorrhoae in the present study.

Introduction

From ancient times, people have sought out drugs that would furnish pleasure and satisfaction, allay anxiety or influence the psyche in other ways considered desirable. Among these agents, some induced the physical dependence to the users (Avram, Lewis and Summer, 1974). Pentazocine is am important agent of this new millennium due to its psychotamimetic effects such as uncontrollable thought, anxiety, nightmares, hallucination and euphoria (Krantz and Carr, 1969; Goodman and Gilman, 1985).

Pentazocine is a synthetic agonist-antagonist compound of analgesicopioid drug which is having the structure of morphine skeleton, replaced of ring C by methyl group with lacked of ether bridge in dimethylallyl at N-atom (Clouet, 1971; Goodman and Gilman, 1985).

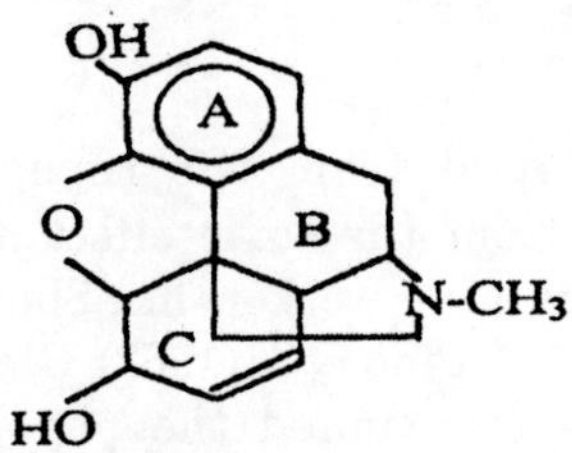

Morphine

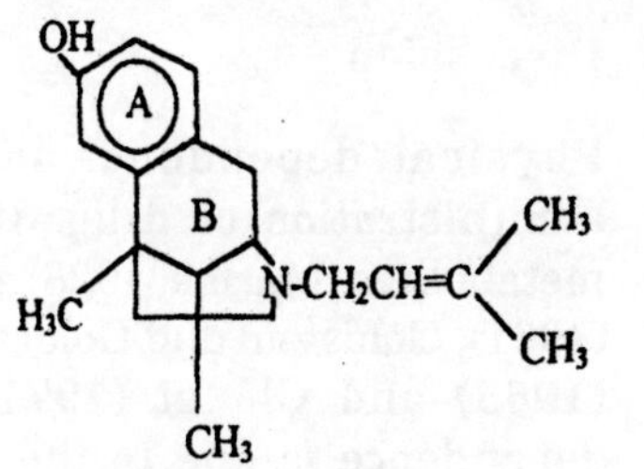

Pentazocine

The present study is an endeavour to highlight the pentazocine induced physical dependence based on the observation of loss of body weight, elevation of body temperature, lachrymation and rhinorrhoae after abruptly removed of pentazocine.

Experimental

Seven groups of albino rats each comprising of five rats were chosen for the present investigation. They were fed regularly with balance diet and water (Farris, 1954) to avoid the stress of starvation. Thus, the animals were acclimatized to laboratory conditions for three weeks prior to the study.

Group one was kept as control where as groups two to seven were administered pentazocine with daily does of 0.05 mg $100gm^{-1}$ (½ Ed_{50}) for the periods of 30, 60, 90, 120, 150, and 180 days respectively. After completion of above periods poentazocine administration was stopped abruptly and the animals were observed for the physiological change i.e. body weight, body temperature, lachrymation and rhinorrhoae.

1. Weight: it was measured with suitable physical balance.
2. Temperature: The body temperature was noted at rectum with digital thermometer.
3. Lachrymation and Rhinorrhoae was observed by general gross observation method.

Results

The detailed results of the present study are shown in Table 1 to 4.

Discussion

Physical dependence is developed from the repeated administration of drug. It may from the toxic effect of it metabolites (Marme, 1928) and some other workers like Shuster (1961), Goldstein and Goldstein (1961), Piha *et.al* (1963), Glasky (1963) and Clouet (1971) were mentioned the physical dependence is due to the alternation of biochemical.

The observation Table 1 shows that, the body weight of experimental animals before drug administration, during pentazocine treatment and during withdrawal of pentazocine administration. The experimental rats have not significant loss of body weight after abruptly suspended of pentazocine administration.

There is no significant elevation of rectal temperature during the pentazocine withdrawal was shown in Table 2.

The number of lachrymation responding rats was shown in Table 3. Only a few number of animals have lachrymation during the pentazocine administration. It may be due to pain fro irritation, at injection site, by presence of lactic acid in the pentazocine injection from (Goodman and Gilman, 1985). There is no lachrymation among the withdrawal animals.

Similarly, a few number of experimental animals have the symptom of rhinorrhoae during the pentazocine administration (Table 4). It may fro the toxic action of pentazocine. The withdrawal of chronic pentazocine administration.

These results are in accordance to neuschatz (1969) work. He reported that, there is no physical dependence when the pentazocine was withdrawal from single dose administration up to 6 months.

REFERENCES

1. Avram, Goldstein: Lewis, Aronow and Summer, M. Kalman: *Principle of Drug Action,* 2nd ed. John Wiley and Sons, New York, (1974).
2. Clouet, Doris H.; *Narcotic Drugs: Biochemical Pharmacology,* 2nd printing, Plenum Press, New York, (1971).
3. Faris, J. Edmand: *the Care and Breeding of Laboratory Animals,* John Wiley and Sons, Inc. New York, (1954).
4. Glasky, A.J.; *Fed. Proc.,* 22, 272 (1963).
5. Goldstein, D.B. and Goldstein, A., *Biochem. Pharmacol.,* 8, 48-49 (1961).
6. Goodman, L.S. and Gilman, A.G.; *The Phramacological Basis of Therapeutics,* 7th ed. Macmillan, London (1985), pp. 520-522.
7. Krantz, John C. and Carr, Jallett; *Pharmacologic Principle of Medical Pratice,* 7th ed. William and Willkins Company, Clacutta (1969), pp. 157-158.
8. Marme, W.; The Opium Problem, p. 362, *Committee on Drug Addiction and bureau on Social Hygiene,* New York (1928).
9. Neuschatz, J. (Letter), *J.Am. Med. Ass.* 209, 112, (1969).
10. Piha, *et.al; Ann Med. Exp. Fenn.,* 41, 498 (1963).
11. Shuster, L.; *Nature 189,* 314-315 (1961).

Table 1
Influence on ody Weight of Albino Rat After Termination of Chronic Pentazocine Administration

Dose : 0.05 mg 100 gm^{-1} day^{-1} N=5

Day	Body weight (gm.) of the experimental animals								
	Before drug administration	During drug administration	During drug termination						
			1st day	2nd day	3rd day	4th day	5th day	6th day	7th day
30days	162.80 ±6.53	162.80 ±7.00 P*	162.60 ±6.82 P*	162.60 ±6.95 P*	162.80 ±6.09 P*	162.80 ±6.17 P*	163.00 ±6.30 P*	163.00 ±6.15 P*	163.33 ±6.47 P*
60 days	157.75±6.42	158.40±6.55 P*	158.40±6.50 P*	158.40±6.68 P*	158.40±6.54 P*	158.60±6.24 P*	158.60±6.47 P*	158.75±6.00 P*	158.79±6.16 P*
90days	162.60±7.52	162.52±7.30 P*	162.45±7.28 P*	162.45±7.61 P*	162.50±7.49 P*	162.50±7.53 P*	162.55±7.00 P*	162.70±7.01 P*	162.70±7.13 P*
120days	185.55±5.63	185.20±5.85 P*	185.20±5.74 P*	185.20±5.84 P*	185.60±5.35 P*	185.60±5.39 P*	185.71±5.42 P*	185.72±5.15 P*	185.85±5.55 P*
150 days	179.78±6.22	179.40±6.47 P*	179.40±6.50 P*	179.40±6.68 P*	179.70±6.29 P*	179.70±6.50 P*	180.00±6.39 P*	180.00±6.40 P*	180.52±6.70 P*
180 days	184.35±6.27	183.75±5.35 P*	183.70±5.28 P*	183.80±5.33 P*	183.80±5.49 P*	184.00±5.38 P*	184.00±5.25 P*	184.22±5.50 P*	184.25±5.45 P*

P* = Not Significant

Table 2

Influence on Boy Temperature of Albino Rat After Termination of Chronic Pentazocine Administration

Dose : 0.05 mg 100 gm^{-1} day^{-1} N=5

Day	Rectal Temperature (°F.) of the experimental animals								
	Before drug administration	During drug administration	During drug termination						
			1st day	2nd day	3rd day	4th day	5th day	6th day	7th day
30days	95.5 ±0.37	95.8 ±0.33 P*	95.8 ±0.40 P*	95.7 ±0.46 P*	95.5 ±0.42 P*	95.6 ±0.31 P*	95.5 ±0.28 P*	95.5 ±0.37 P*	95.5 ±0.37 P*
60 days	95.6 ±0.32	95.0 ±0.37 P*	95.9 ±0.35 P*	95.8 ±0.35 P*	95.6 ±0.36 P*	95.5 ±0.36 P*	95.5 ±0.34 P*	95.6 ±0.35 P*	95.5 ±0.33 P*
90days	95.6 ±0.35	96.2 ±0.34 P*	96.2 ±0.32 P*	95.8 ±0.32 P*	96.0 ±0.32 P*	95.5 ±0.39 P*	95.5 ±0.39 P*	95.6 ±0.36 P*	95.6 ±0.28 P*
120days	95.5 ±0.37	96.2 ±0.43 P*	96.2 ±0.41 P*	96.0 ±0.45 P*	95.7 ±0.38 P*	95.5 ±0.34 P*	95.7 ±0.37 P*	95.5 ±0.36 P*	95.5 ±0.38 P*
150 days	95.4 ±0.45	96.3 ±0.32 P*	96.4 ±0.38 P*	96.3 ±0.46 P*	96.0 ±0.35 P*	96.1 ±0.40 P*	95.5 ±0.36 P*	95.4 ±0.34 P*	95.6 ±0.35 P*
180 days	95.5 ±0.37	96.2 ±0.43 P*	96.2 ±0.40 P*	96.4 ±0.45 P*	96.0 ±0.44 P*	96.2 ±0.40 P*	95.8 ±0.37 P*	95.8 ±0.37 P*	95.4 ±0.38 P*

P* = Not Significant

Table 3
Influence on Lachrymation of Albino Rat After Termination of Chronic Pentazocine Administration

Day	*Numer of Animal responding to Lachrymation*								
	Before drug adminis-tration	*During drug adminis-tration*	*During drug termination*						
			1st day	*2nd day*	*3rd day*	*4th day*	*5th day*	*6th day*	*7th day*
30days	0	0	0	0	0	0	0	0	0
60 days	0	1	0	0	0	0	0	0	0
90 days	0	0	0	0	0	0	0	0	0
120 days	0	0	0	0	0	0	0	0	0
150 days	0	1	0	0	0	0	0	0	0
180 days	0	1	0	0	0	0	0	0	0

Table 4
Influence on Rhinorrhoae of Albino Rat After Termination of Chronic Pentazocine Administation

Day	*Numer of Animal responding to Lachrymation*								
	Before drug administration	*During drug administration*	*During drug termination*						
			1st day	*2nd day*	*3rd day*	*4th day*	*5th day*	*6th day*	*7th day*
30days	0	0	0	0	0	0	0	0	0
60 days	0	0	0	0	0	0	0	0	0
90 days	0	0	0	0	0	0	0	0	0
120 days	0	1	0	0	0	0	0	0	0
150 days	0	0	0	0	0	0	0	0	0
180 days	0	1	0	0	0	0	0	0	0

10

Crimes Against Women and Role of Forensic Science

*Bindu Variath**

Introduction

Women are the symbol of unfathomable depths of human sentiments, manifestations of unstable heights of selfless affection and sacrifice. They are the evolutionary unmatchable creators of mortality, religious sentiments, cultural upheavals, imagery, idealism and spiritualism. Women are the personification of happiness, tenderness, solace and power. They are the embodiment of kindness, sympathy and modesty.

Tracing back the history, the cross road landmarks speak about the humiliation, torture and exploitation of women. Women of India have been bearing the cross right before their birth till their last breath. The gender bias dogs them all through their life, making them virtual lesser species and second class citizens. Even thought the society claims of the civilization, in all conceivable fields, the realms of science and technology, information technology, space science green evolution, genetic engineering and the like, in the

* Lecturer, Institute of Law, Budelkhand University, Jhansi.

vital measurement of human progress we seem to be deliberately sidelining half of humanity—women. Gross discrimination apart, women are being subjected to a plethora of atrocities and a virtual denial of basic human rights. It is said that all rights of women are human rights, but in reality bulk of our women are denied basic human rights just because they happen to be women.

The various types of atrocities against women are dowry harassment, trafficking of girls and women, molestation, kidnapping and abduction, sexual harassment, gang rape, commercializing femininity for sex, eve-teasing, organizational cabaret for exhibitionistic nudity and so forth. Due to the increasing number of cruelties against women year by year now it has reached in such a situation that atrocities of against women start even before they are born.

Lakhs of parents, in their eagerness to have son only, get rid of daughters through sex determination tests, indulging in the crime of female foeticide. So now it has led to the fall in the male-female sex ratio. In the changed political economy of both values and technology female infanticide has given to female foeticide.

There is mushroom growth of profit making industries of sex determination tests. As a result female child is not allowed to be born. The supreme court has taken note of sharp decline in the sex ratio and have given direction to the union and state government to implemented the Pre-natal Diagnostic Techniques (Regulation and prevention of misuses) Act and to launch a mass awareness campaign to enlighten the people towards its disadvantages.

Dowry Deaths

One of the greatest atrocities, women are facing today, despite legislation and the spread of education, is dowry, a social evil that is growing day by day. Women are being sacrificed at the altar of dowry and are being burnt alive with the convenience of the husband and in-laws. The custom of dowry is deep rooted in Indian society but over the years it has turned into a social menace, too entrenched and diabolical to be tackled by reformers and law makers. So many efforts for the eradication of the dowry practice was taken but still perhaps it has become the most alarming social issue in the present country. According to the National Commission for women (NCW) the crime graph against women continues to be on the upswing. Dowry in its original form, was not based on a avarice and extortion as is quite often the case today but was just a token of love and regard for the bridegroom.

Varadakshina, as it was known in the Hindu shastras, was dakshina of a purely voluntary nature without which the meritorious act of kanyadaan would not be complete. Religious rationalization apart, the main motivation on the part of the bride's parents was to provide security and compensation for inheritance rights to the daughter in order to enable her to led a harmonious relationship with her husband and his family. Gradually, the element of voluantariness disappeared and a callous, crass and commercial system came into being.

Sexual Offences

There are various types of sexual offences against women like rape, prostitution, abortion sexual abuse of child etc. now the situation is that no place and no time is safe for the women neither her home nor place of work, the crowed streets or claustrophobic space can provide her safety. Every minor girl become easy victims of rapists. Most of the victims of rape has to keep the mouth shut because they are ashamed of whether the society would tease them and they have to carry the stigma of rape all through their life. The victims are punished in manifold ways, and they also have to prove to the court that they did not consent to itself is as in human to the victims of rape. The laws relating to rape has to be reviewed and more punishment should be given other wise the number of unwed mothers will go on increasing.

Sati and Stigma of Widowhood

The next is sati. The fact is that practice of sati has become extremely rape in contemporary Hindu society, an appraisal of issues is warranted in view of the social values, the diabolical nature of the practice, extreme cruelty involved and some shocking incidents in the very recent past. Sati in Sanskrit, means a noble and dedicated wife. When applied to a widow, the word stands for a women voluntarily sacrificing herself of the funeral pyre of her husband, the act of self-immolation being an expression of love for the husband.

The practice is believed to be based on ancient Hindu shastras and scriptures which prescribed it is means to attain spiritual purity. It was also regarded as the infliction of natural punishment for the sins committed in the earlier life by the women.

Emile Durkheim and some other sociologist regarded sati as a religious suicide. Whatever the original motivations, sati practice, in course of time, assumed an altogether different character. In a gruesome sati reported from Puna in 1823, the women escaped from the pyre twice, and though excessively burnt plunged herself into the river. She was caught by a number of persons who hit her mercilessly with billets. After being rescued by two Englishmen she died in hospital, the last word uttered by her was 'save me from death.' Sati committed by a young Rajput girl in a village of Rajasthan shaked the entire country leading to the enactment of the Sati (Prevention) Act, 1987. The various other types of atrocities against women are trafficking of girls and women, molestation, kidnapping and abduction etc.

Provision in Indian Constitution

Provision in Indian constitution and certain other legislations are giving certain special care and attention and relaxation for women. In the Indian constitution Article 15(3) empower the state of make special provisions for women and children. The reason is that "women's physical structure and the performance of material functions place her at a disadvantage in the struggle for subsistence and their physical well-being becomes an object of public interest, land care and in order to preserve the strength and vigour of the race. (Muller, V. Oregon, 52, L-Ed. 551). Thus under article 42 women worker can be given special maternity relief and a law to this effect will not infringe Article 15 (1). Again it would not be violation of Article 15 if educational institutions are established by the state exclusively for women. The reservation of seats for women in a college does not offend against Article 15 (1). Section 497 of Indian Penal Code punishes only men for adultery and exempts the women from punishment even though she may be equally guilty as an abettor was held to be valid since the classification was not based on the ground of sex alone, Yusuf Abdul Aziz V State of Bombay AIR 1954 H.SC 321. There are certain other provisions in the directive principles also which is giving special consideration for women and children.

Role of Human Rights

Human Rights are those rights which are inherent in our nature and without which we can not live as human beings. Human Rights and fundamental freedoms allows us develop fully and use human qualities, our intelligence, our talents, and our conscience and to satisfy our spiritual and other needs. They are based on mankind's increasing demand for a life in which the inherent dignity and worth of each human being will receive respect and protection.

The denial of human rights and fundamental freedom is not only an individual and personal tragedy, but also creates conditions and social and political unrest, sowing the seeds of evidence and conflict within the between societies and nations. The first sentence of the universal declaration of human rights stases, respect of human rights and human dignity is the foundation of freedom, justice and peace in the world. Taking into consideration of all types of discrimination torture etc. against the women human rights has taken steps to eliminate all the types of violence against women.

There is a separate convention for women's right known a Convention on the Elimination of all forms of Discrimination against its object is to implement equality between men and women and to prevent discrimination against women, in particular such as specific forms of discrimination as forced marriage, domestic violence and less access to education, health care and public life as well as discrimination at work.

Role of Forensic Science

In spite of the stringent provision of law with respect to the punishment, appreciation and adducing of evidence etc., a lion share of dowry related cases go unconvicted.

The main reason for this phenomenon is the lack of insufficiency of direct and independent evidence. All most all the murders related to dowry take place in the matrimonial home. That is the house where the victims living with her husband and in laws. Before such a murder or dowry related death or suicide take place, the victim will be subjected to long and continuous physical and mental harassment. It is the destiny of the poor bride to bear with the torture for a long time in silence. At the most she would be able to inform her parents, especially the mother. The natural and initial reaction of the parents would be either an advice to bear it patiently or in some cases they too would be putting the blame on her, it makes her even more helpless.

When a tragic end comes to the suffering of the bride, in the form of a murder, suicide or unnatural death, the availability of immediate eye witness is a remote possibility. The inmates of matrimonial home i.e. the relative of the husband stand more as accused than as witness. More ever prosecution can not expect anyone in the house to come forward and give evidence against the accused. Next comes the neighbours, knowing the under currents of the house is also remote. Apart from this many of the neighbours would not like to antagonise others by giving evidence against them. Even if some volunteer to come foreword for giving evidence out of an emotional outbreak at the time of the occurrence, they may turn hostile at the trial stage.

No doubt there are some exception to the above. But by and large what stated above is true. So adducing independent and direct evidence in dowry death cases is a very difficult task and a major handicap to the prosecution.

So the prosecution has to rely upon the circumstantial evidence in such cases. Here the Forensic Science Department has to play a crucial role. The investing agency shall effectively utilize the service of Forensic Science Department in collecting evidence.

Collecting Scientific evidence shall start from the scene of occurrence. The scene of occurrence will have to be preserved unaltered and undisturbed, for the examination by experts. In almost all the cases vital clues will be available from the scene itself. That would include burn remains, external object in the place of occurrence such as rope, weapons, chappals, piece of cloth, other material objects used for the crime such as bottles or canes of fuel poison etc.

The next important aspect is the examination of the body of the victims and to trace the pre-mortum injuries or marks on the body of the victims must be put to scientific test so as to support the prosecution cases.

Another and most important aspect is the examination of internal cases of the victims after the post-mortum. But out investigating agencies are not making use of this facility in many cases of poisoning, drawing damage of internal organs due to physical torture etc.

Scientific examination of materials like hair, blood stains on the clots, and on other objects, finger prints on the body of the victim, finger print on material objects like weapons, the wall, furniture etc., on the place of occurrence, foot marks in and a around the place of occurrence, hand writing and signature on suspected documents, letters, suicides notes etc. will provide vital clues to the investigation.

In all these cases, utmost caution and adherence to the scientific methods shall be observed at all levels of collecting sample, preservation of sample foe examination, preparation of report and so on.

The officials in the police department must be trained adequately so as to create an awareness with respect to the need of collecting and making use of scientific evidences in these cases. Like wise the forensic science officials must also be trained on different aspects related to the principles involved in adducing evidence by the prosecution appreciation of evidence by the courts and the methods followed by police in the course of their investigation and position of law in respect of all these aspects. To conclude, there, must be greater co-operation and co-ordination among the agencies like the forensic science Dept. the police, and the prosecution to secure effective and meaningful prosecution of dowry related crimes.

Above all there must be a social education by scholars, social and voluntary organisation, lawyers, political parties, religious leaders and women's organisations to treat dowry as a social evil and to eradicate it from the society.

BIBLIOGRAPHY

1. Siddiqe Ahamad, *Criminology Problems and Perspectives,* 2001.
2. Ratanlal and Dhirjlal, *The Indian Penal Code,* Reprint, 2000.
3. Dr. T. Bhattacharya, *The Indian Penal Code,* 3rd edition, 2001.
4. Dr. S.S. Srivastava, *Criminal Law,* 3rd edition, 2001.
5. Ratanlal and Dhirajlal, *The Code of Criminal Procedure,* Reprint, 2001.1
6. Ponnaian, *Criminology,* 1975.
7. Russel, *Criminal Law,* Vol. I (11th edition.)
8. Dr. R.C. Nigam, *Law of Crimes in India,* Vol. I.
9. Kenny, *Outlines of Criminal Law.*
10. Miller, *Handbook of Criminal Law.*

11

Forensic Importance of Insects Sequentially Colonizing Carcasses

*Devinder Singh**

*Meenakshi Bharti***

Decomposing animal carcasses undergo a series of predictable changes during decomposition and are "visited" by a succession of flies and other insects (Goff, 1991). This ordered process has handed us an invaluable tool for estimating the age of cadavers and to make other interpretations of forensic importance. The use of entomological knowledge during crime investigation has resulted in the development of a separate branch of science commonly called Forensic Entomology. It is based on the analysis of those insects that sequentially colonize a corpse as decomposition progresses and on the rate at which various stages of their progeny develop.

The first recorded instance when insects were used to solve crime is from China in the 13th century (McKnight, 1981). Forensic entomology emerged as a major discipline with passage of time in developed countries and its role in investigations about crime has continued to become more and more relevant. Now-a-days, forensic entomologists are

* Department of Zoology, Punjabi University, Patiala-157 002.

** Department of Zoology, Punjabi University, Patiala-157 002.

hired by prosecutors and defenders like lawyers. Even some of the well-known detective agencies like FBI of USA have employed entomologists as special agents. Hundreds of research papers dealing directly or indirectly with forensic entomology have been published so far and this number is increasing day by day. Four books dealing solely with forensic entomology are now available. These are: "A Manual of Forensic Entomology" by Smith (1986), "Entomology and Death: A Procedural Guide" by Catts and Haskell (1990),, "A Fly for the prosecution: how insect evidence helps solve crime" by Goff (2000) and "Forensic Entomology. The utility of arthropods in legal investigations" by Byrd and Castner (2000).

Forensic cntomology proceeds on the common observation that exposed animal remains present a temporary and progressively changing habitat and food source for a wide variety of organisms ranging from microbes like bacteria and fungi to vertebrate scavengers. Out of these, arthropod fauna comprises a major element of the biota and insects form the most constant, diverse and conspicuous group. These six-legged creatures predominate the terrestrial and fresh water carrion fauna. Payne (1965) reported 522 species of animals from decomposing pig carcasses out of which 84% were insects. During our studies on decomposing rabbit carcasses, 38 insect species were recorded. These insects are attracted, in the first instance, to the body fluids oozing from natural openings and to blood or serum escaping from the wounds. Out of all the insects collected during the present studies, 55% belonged to Diptera and 21% were coleopterans. These insects form a complex food web within the carrion. This web gets more complicated because of the fact that many species have different adult food preferences from that of their larvae. The carrion insects can be grouped into following categories on the basis of their food preferences that also reflect their ecological role.

1. *Necrophagous species:* These species feed on corpse tissue and are further subdivided into three categories.

   (a) Sarcosaprophages: These species feed on decomposing flesh and this group also includes

arthropods which imbibe blood or the fluids that bathe the tissue as thin film e.g. Calliphoridae, Sarcophagidae, Muscidae, Dermestidae.

(b) Coprophages: Species that are attracted to the rumen contents of herbivorous mammals e.g. Scarabaeidae and Muscidae.

(c) Dermatophates: Species feeding on dried skin, hair, ligament and bones e.g. Dermestidae, Tineidae.

2. *Necrophagous-predaceous species:* Insects that feed on corpse and its inhabitants e.g,. Ants (Formicidae), silphid beetles, clerid beetles and some blow fly larvae (*Chrysomya rufifacies*).
3. *Predaceous Species:* Arthropods that feed only on carrion entomofauna, especially dipterous larvae e.g. Histeridae, Stayphylinidae.
4. *Parasitic species:* Insects that parasitize fly larvae and pupae e.g. endoparasitic wasps.
5. *Adventive or incidental species:* Arthropods that use carrion as a concentrated resource extension of their normal habitat e.g. spiders, centipedes, millipedes, mites etc.

Out of all the insects visiting dead bodies, the maggots of blowflies (Calliphoridae) and flesh flies (Sacrophagidae) are responsible for the maximum carrion consumption in a terrestrial environment (Fuller, 1934; Payne, 1965; Putman, 1977 and 1978; Braack, 1981; Early and Goff, 1986). Adults of these flies use carrion for feeding, mating and breeding. Blow flies lay eggs while flesh flies deposit larvae in natural body orifices and these larvae quickly invade most of the regions of the animal body (Putman, 1978). The proteolytic enzymes in the larval excreta poured directly into the carrion material further aids in liquefaction of the carcass. The mechanical action of their tunneling through the tissue increases aeration and helps in dissemination of microorganisms. So both these mechanisms initiated by dipteran larvae serve to increase microbial activity and hasten rate of decomposition. Payne (1965) observed that pig carcasses left uncovered and freely exposed to insects lost upto 90% of their weight within one week during summer month in contrast to screened carcasses made inaccessible to insects which gradually dried out over a period for 100 days.

During its decomposition and age in the carrion passes through a series of characteristic physical and chemical changes and in the absence of vertebrate scavengers, a temporal heterotypic succession of arthropod species occurs (Hanski, 1987). While decomposition is a continuous process, many workers have divided it into separate successive stages for better understanding. These are fresh, bloated, decay and dry stages.

(a) *Fresh stage:* This stage begins at the moment of death and ends when bloating is first evident. The first organisms to arrive at the remains are the flies belonging to the families Calliphoridae (blowflies) and Sarcophagidae (flesh flies). Larvae or eggs are deposited around the natural body openings associated with the head and urino genital regions.

(b) *Bloated stage:* Putrefaction, the principal component of decomposition, begins during this stage. Gases produced by the metabolic activities of anaerobic bacteria first cause a slight inflation of the abdomen and the corpse may later assume a fully inflated, balloon like appearance. Internal carcass temperatures begin to rise during this stage as a combined result of the putrefaction processes and the metabolic activities of dipteran larvae. Calliphoridae are strongly attracted to remains during this stage, reaching the greatest numbers at the peak of inflation. Fluids seeping from natural body openings during this stage combined with ammonia produced through the metabolic activities of dipteran larvae cause the soil beneath the carcass to become alkaline. Normal soil fauna will depart the area beneath the remains during this stage.

(c) *Decay stage:* This is the only stage having a distinct physical event marking the starting point. It is considered to begin when skin is broken, allowing gases to escape and the remains deflate. Dipteran larvae forming large feeding masses are the predominant taxa present during this stage. Coleopterans also arrive during the decay stage. Both necrophagous and predatory taxa are observed in large numbers during the later portions of this stage. By the end of this stage most members of Calliphoridae and Sarcophagidae complete their larval development and depart from the remains for pupariation. The carrion temperature during this stage is considerably higher than the soil temperature (Payne, 1965) and even higher than the surrounding air temperature (Williams and Richardson, 1984; Introna *et. al,* 1989; Turner and Howard, 1992). Early and Goff (1986) and Tullis and Goff (1987) recorded differences upto 22°C between carcass temperature and ambient air temperature. In the Present study, carrion temperature was recorded as high as 10°C above ambient during this stage. Payne (1965) observed that fly maggots consumed 90% of the carcass biomass by the end of this stage and this was observed to be so during the present study as well.

(d) *Dry stage:* This is the final stage of decomposition. The carcass consists of only dry skin, fur, cartilage and bones. Internal carcass temperature approximates that of ambient (Early and Goff, 1986). The end of this stage is difficult to define as noted by various authors due to its long duration and lack of pronounced marking events. However, Reed (1958) stated that this stage might last upto a point when no carrion fauna remains.

While carrion is often rich in species diversity, only some are true carrion feeders and have significant role in the decomposition and release of carrion materials. These are mainly the fly maggots and dermestid beetles (Putman, 1983). Information about the entomofauna of a decaying deed body can be useful during forensic investigations in several ways.

Time of Death: There are two basic approaches to the application of entomological data for estimating the time of death. During earlier stages of decomposition, the time elapsed since death or post-mortem internal (PMI) may be determined by calculating the time required for a given species to reach the particular stage of development recovered from the corpse at the time of discovery. The insects involved in this approach are mostly dipterans, especially those belonging to families Calliphrodae and Sarcophagidae. The most advanced stage of development that in turn shows the longest period of association with the corpse is used to estimate the minimum possible PMI. After the initial stages of decomposition are over and when the Calliphoridae and Sarcophagidae have departed, estimates are generally based on the interpretations of arthropod succession patterns because different types of insects colonize dead bodies at different stages of decay.

Mode of Death: A dead body having external injuries is more attractive to insects than one having none. So, depending upon the degree of degradation brought about by maggots, an entomologist may be able to suggest the possible mode of death e.g. strangulation or mutilation (Anderson, 1997). Another application is in the cases where death has occurred due to the intake of drugs. A chemical analysis of the maggots found on the dead body can reveal specific drugs, especially helpful when no human tissues are available for sending to the laboratory for chemical tests. During experimental studies large number of poisonous chemicals have been recovered from maggots that were allowed to feed upon animals that died due to intake of such chemicals. To name few, cocaine (Goff *et. at,* 1989), trizolam, oxazepam, alimemazine, chloripriamine and phenobari\bital (Kintz *et. al,* 1990a, 1990b and 1990c) methamphetamine (Goff *et. al,* 1992), lead arsenate (Leclerq and Valliant, 1992), coproxamol and amitriptyline (Wilson *et. al,* 1993) have been recovered from maggot tissues.

Place of Death: The deceased may have been killed at a place other than where the body is found. With knowledge about the carrion fauna of an area and specific habits of species found on the cadaver, an entomologist can help determine whether the person died at a place other than where the body has been found. Similarly, route of transport of a dead body may also be traced by using entomological data.

There are numerous other special situations where entomologists can help to solve crime. If a body is found buried in soil, the entomological data can be helpful in determining the period intervening death and burial (Lord *et. al,* 1992). Blowfly larvae found in the diapers have been used to provide information on how long children had been neglected by their parents (Lord, 1990).

The about presented text gives a fair idea about the potential importance of insect evidence during forensic investigations. However, a detailed knowledge about the carrion fauna of the specific area with respect to life history, habits, geographical distribution, taxonomy, morphology of immature stages, ecological relations etc. is a must for the use of these insects in solving crime.

REFERENCES

Anderson, G.S., 1997. The use of insects to determine time of decapitation: A case study from British Columbia. *J. Forens. Sci.,* 41(4): 617-625.

Braack, L.E.O., 1981. Visitation pattern of principal species of the insect complex at carcasses in the Kruger National Park. *Koedoe,* 24: 33-49.

Byrd, J.H. and Castner, J.L., 2000. *The utility of arthropods in legal investigations.* Florida: CRC Press.

Catts, E.P. and Haskell, N.H., 1992. *Entomology and Death: A procedural guide.* Clemson, SC: Joyce's Print Shop.

Early, M. and Goff, M.L., 1986. Arthropod succession patterns in exposed carrion on the island of O'ahu, Hawaiian Islands, USA. *J. Med. Entomol.,* 23(5): 520-531.

Fuller, M.E., 1934. The insect inhabitants of carrion, a study in animal ecology. *Bull. Council Sci. Indi. Res.,* Melbourne, 82: 5-62.

Goff, M.L., 1991. Feast of clues: insects in the service of forensics. *The Sciences:* 3035.

Goff, M.L., 2000. *A fly for the prosecution: How insect evidence helps solving crime.* London: Harvard University Press.

Goff, M.L., Omori, A.I. and Goodbroad, J.R. 1989. Effect of cocain in tissues on the development rate of *boettcherisca peregrine* (Diptera: Sacrophagidae). *J. Med. Entomol.,* 26(2): 91-93.

Goff, M.L., Brown, W.A. and Omori, A.L., 1992. Preliminary observations on the development rate of *Parasarcophage ruficornis* (Diptera: Sarcophagidae) and implications of this effect on the estimations of post-mortem intervals. *J. Forens. Sci.,* 37(3): 867-872.

Hanski, I., 1987. In *Colonization, Succession and stability.* A.J. Grey, M.J. Crawley and P.J. Edwards (eds.), London: Black Well Scientific Publications.

Introna, F., Altamura, B.M., Delle'Erba, A. and Dattoli, V. 1989. Time since death definition by experimental reproduction of *Lucilia sericata* cycles in growth cabinet. *Forens. Sci.,* 34: 478-480.

Kintz, P., Tracqui, A., Ludes, B., Waller, J., Bonkhabza, A., Mangin, P., Lugnier, A.A. and Chaumont, A.J. 1990b. Fly larvae and their relevance in forensic toxicology. *Am. J. Forens. Med. Pathol.,* 11(1): 63-65.

Kintz, P., Tracqui, A. and Mangin, P. 1990c. Toxicology and fly larvae on a putrefied cadaver. *J. Forens. Sci. Soc.,* 30(4): 243-246.

Leclercq, M. and Valliant, F. 1992. Entomologie et medicine legale: unc observation inedited *Ann. Soc. Ent. Fr. (N.S.),* 28(1): 3-8.

Lord, W.D. 1990. In *Entomology and Death: A procedural guide,* E.P. Catts and N.H. Haskell (eds.), Joyce's Print shop, Clemson.

Lord, W.D., Edkis, T.R. and Catts, E.P. 1992. The use of *Synthesiomyia nudesita* (Van Der Wulp) (Diptera; Muscidae) and *Calliphora vicina* (Robineau-Desvoidy) (Diptera: Calliphoridae) to estimate the time of death of a body buried under a house. *J. Agric. Entomol.,* 9(4): 227-235.

McKnight, B.E. 1981. *The washing away of wrongs: Forensic Medicine in Thirteenth-Century China,* Trans. Ann. Arbor: Univ. Michigan.

Payne, J.A. 1965. A summer carrion study of the baby pig *Sus scrofa* Linnaeus. *Ecology,* 46(5): 592-602.

Putman, R.J. 1977. Dynamics of the blowfly *Calliphora erythrocephala* within carrion. *J. Anim. Ecol.,* 46: 853-866.

Putman, R.J. 1978. The role of carrion frequenting arthropods int eh decay process. *Ecol. Entomol.,* 3: 133-139.

Putman, R.J. 1983. *Carrion and Dung: THe decomposition of animal wates.* London: Edward Arnold.

Reed, H.B. 1958. A study of dog carcass communities in Tennessee, with special reference to the insects. *Am. Midle. Nat.,* 59(1): 213-245.

Smith, K.G.V. 1986. *A manual of forensic entomology.* New York: Comstock Publishing Associates.

Tullis, K. and Goff, M.L. 1987. Arthropod succession in exposed carrion in a tropical rain forest on O'ahu Island, Hawaii. *J. Med. Entomol.,* 24: 332-339.

Turner, B.D. and Howard, T. 1992. Metabolic heat generation in dipteran larval aggregations: A consideration for forensic entomology. *Med. Vet. Entomol.,* 6: 179-181.

Williams, H. and Richardson, A.M. 1984. Growth energetics in relation to temperature for larvae of four species of necrophagous flies (Diptera: Calliphoridae). *Aust. J. Ecol.,* 9: 141-152.

Wilson, Z., Hubbard, S. and Pounder, D.J. 1993. Drug analysis in fly larvae. *Am. J. Forens. Med. Path.,* 14(2): 118-120.

12

Pattern Recognition

*Yashpal Singh**

*Aditya Chaturvedi***

*Priyank Tripathi****

*Ankur Katiyar*****

Abstract

This paper primarily focuses on the new advents of pattern recognition techniques, which are reforming the research fields of communication and forensic sciences. Pattern recognition adopts various algorithms—Back propagation training algorithm takes the backdrop of computational statistical pattern recognition and neural networking methods, Support Vector Machines (SVM) is a relatively novel pattern recognition approach based on the theory of underlying statistical learning, specially the Structural Risk Minimization (SRM), Principal Components Analysis (PCA) is commonly used in many fields including feature extraction and data compression, Independent Component as Analysis (ICA) is a new technique commonly used in blind source separation where higher-order statistics of the data are important.

---

*, **, ***, **** Maithilisharn Gupt Bundelkhand Institute of Engineering & Technology Jhansi 284 001.

Introduction

Pattern recognition is the recognition or separation of one particular sequence of bits or pattern from other such patterns. Pattern Recognition [PR] applications have been varied, and, so also the associated data structures and processing paradigms. Four significant approaches to PR have evolved. These are:

- *Statistical Pattern Recognition:* Here, the problem is posed as one of composite hypothesis testing, each hypothesis pertaining to the premise, of the datum having originated from a particular class; or as one of regression from the space of measurements to the space of classes. The statistical approach is one of the oldest, and still widely used.
- *Syntactic Pattern Recognition:* In syntactic pattern recognition, each pattern is assumed to be composed of sub-patterns or primitives strung together in accordance with the generation rules of a grammar characteristic of the associated class.
- *Knowledge-based Pattern Recognition:* This approach to PR has evolved from advance in rule-based system in artificial intelligence (AI). Each rule is in form of a clause that reflects evidence about the presence of a particular class.
- *Neural Pattern Recognition:* Artificial Neural Network (ANN) provides an emerging paradigm in pattern recognition. The field of ANN encompasses a large variety of models, all of which have two important characteristics:
    1. They are composed of a large no. of structurally and functionally similar units called Neurons usually connected in various configurations by weighted links.
    2. The ANN model parameters are derived from supplied I/O paired data sets by an estimation process called *Training.*

Algorithms for Pattern Recognition

There are several algorithms in existence that are being presently used for pattern recognition application. These algorithms vary in their complexities, field of usage and time when they were founded. In this paper, we are going to discuss four of them, namely:

1. Back Propagation Training Algorithm using Neural Networks.
2. Support Vector Machines
3. PCA (Principal Component Analysis), and,
4. ICA (Independent Component Analysis)

We would detail them in the same order.

Back Progatation Training Algorithm

Neural networks are built from simple units called neurons by analogy with the human brain. These units are connected by a set of weighted connections. Neural network learning is usually performed by a modification of the connection weights between units. The units are organized in layers. The first layer is called the input layer, the last one the output layer. Intermediate layers are called the hidden layers and resulting network is called multi-layer perception (Figure 1). The information to be analyzed is first presented to the neurons in the input layer and then propagated to the second layer for further processing. The result of this processing is propagated to the next layer and so on until the last—output layer.

The back-propagation algorithm is a gradient descent method minimizing the mean square error between the actual and target output of a multiplayer perception. Assuming sigmoidal non-linearity.

$$f\text{tnet}_i{}^{1} \frac{1}{1e^{act}} \qquad (5)$$

the back-propagation algorithm consists of the following steps:

1. Initialize Weights and Offsets

Initialize all weights and node offsets to small random values.

2. Present Input and Desired Output Vector

Present continuous input vector x and specify and desired output d. Out put vector elements are set to zero values except for that corresponding to the class of the current input.

3. Calculate Actual Outputs

Calculate the actual output vector y using the sigmoidal non-linearity.

4. Adapt weights

Adjust Weights by

$$w_{if}^{nt} \quad (1) \quad wif^{(t)} \quad \eta \delta_j æ_i \qquad (6)$$

Where X is the output of the node δj and i is the sensitivity of the node j.

If node j is an output node, then

$$\delta j = \text{finet}_j \quad wd_j \quad y_j y \qquad (7)$$

where d_j is the desired output of the node j, y_j is the actual output and is the derivation of the activation function calculated at net_j.

If the node j is an internal node, then the sensitivity is defined as

$$\delta j = f(net_j) \quad \frac{\Sigma}{K} \quad \delta_k w_j k \qquad (8)$$

Where k sums over all nodes in the layer above the node j. Update equations are derived using the chain derivation rule applied to the LMS training criterion functions.

Convergence can be faster if a momentum term is added and weight change are smoothed

$$w_{ij}\ (t)\ (1) = w_{ij}\ (1) + \eta\delta_j\chi_j = \delta\ (w_{ij)}\ (i) - w_{ij}\alpha - (1) \quad (9)$$

Where $0<\alpha<1$.

5. *Repeat by Going to Step 2*

The simplest stopping criterion is to end when the change in the training criterion function is smaller then some present value. A better approach is a cross-validation technique, stopping training when the error on a separate validation set reaches a minimum.

Support Vector Machine

SVMs are based on the theory of underlying statistical learning, specially the Structural Risk Minimization (SRMO.

Vapnik first introduced the theory of SVMs based on the principle of Structural Risk Minimization. Intuitively, given the set of samples belonging to two classes, SVMs learn the boundary between these two classes by mapping the input samples to a high dimensional space that separates the samples of the two classes. This hyper plane is chosen such that it leaves the largest fraction of samples of the same class on the same side while maximizing the distance from the closest training samples from each class. This distance is referred to as margin in SVMs literature. The use of the connectionist systems such as neural networks has been limited because of various limitations such as lack of generalization, optimization process and slow convergence. The SVMs have clearly two distinct advantages. Firstly they have an excellent ability to generalize and secondly they do not need any fine-tuning of parameters. SVMs also demonstrate good convergence property.

PCA (Principal Component Analysis):

Principal component analysis is commonly used for feature extraction. According to this technique, the first principal component of a data set is the direction along which there is largest variance over all samples. The basic idea of this technique is that the direction along which there is maximum variation is most likely to contain the information about the class discrimination. Mapping the given data set into this space will make the difference between classes more significant.

PCA maps the data set using an orthoronmal matrix $Y=F^T X$ to the feature space, where X= $[y1, y2, \ldots yn]^T$ is the original data sex, Y= $[y1, y2, \ldots yn]^T$ is the output data set. The Transformation matrix F can be achieved by SF =, where F and L are the eigenvector matrix and the eigenvalue matrix of the covariance matrix S of the source data X. Since F is an orthonormal matrix, in the transformed space, we have

$$|Y|^2= Y^TY \quad X^T\phi\phi^TX= \quad X^TX \quad |X|$$

The Euclidean distance can be used as the measure of the distance between two data.

Only the mean and the covariance will be used to find out the transformation matrix.

ICA (Independent Component Analysis)

Independent Component Analysis is very similar to PCA. Given a data set X= $[x1, x2, \ldots xn]^T$, ICA will find an nXn matrix W, which will minimize the average mutual information of the output matrix Y= $[y1, y2, \ldots yn]^T$. The difference is transformation matrix is not required to be orthogonal. The computation of this transform involves higher-order statistics of the data, so it's well used for problems such as blind source separation where higher-order statistics of the data are important.

Since a closed-form solution is not tractable, we use a stochastic gradient ascent algorithm. The idea is pick a nonlinear function g(u), which has the same covariance matrix as the underlying independent components, maximizing the joint entropy of g(u) will lead to ICA solution. The specific form of the stochastic gradient ascent that is used involves a learning rule that changes weights according to the gradient of the entropy:

$$\nabla W \alpha \frac{\partial H(y)}{\partial w} W^T W = (T) \,\hat{}(yu^T)w$$

in which $\hat{y}u = \frac{\partial\, \partial yi}{\partial\, yi \partial ui} = \frac{\partial}{\partial ui}(T)\frac{\partial yi}{\partial ui}$ is computed

as $\hat{y} = 1\text{-}2yi$, and $yi = (1 + e^{u}i)\text{-}!$

Comparison of Algorithms & Conclusion:

Two main reasons why Neural Networks (NN) are favourite pattern classification tool are, first it has been proved that they can form arbitrarily complex decision regions and second, their parameters can be trained to form the required decision region by back-propagation algorithm. We can see that neural network with the more hidden units tend to over train faster. Results of the experiments are sensitive to the random initialization; the relative difference is error rate is in 20% range. It is necessary to perform many experiments until the optimal neural network structure is found.

SVMs have proven to be successful in many pattern classification problems such as image identification and face recognition. In many of these problems SVMs have outperformed other non-linear classifiers such as artificial neural networks and k-nearest neighbours since these suffer from many deficiencies such as tendency to over fit and slow convergence. The drawback of SVMs is that they are incapable of successfully modelling the time—varying dynamics of the data such as speech.

Both PCA and ICA can improve the performance of data discrimination problem than 1-NNR rules. Ideally, since the transformation matrix that ICA find is not required to be orthogonal, so ICA will give a better result than PCA do. Since ICA uses all order of statistics, it is more useful than PCA while the higher-order statistics of data are important.

REFERENCE

1. Schalkoff R.J., "Pattern Recognition: Statistical Structured and Neural; Approach", John Wiley and Sons, 1992.
2. Fukuanga K., "Statistical Pattern Recognition-2nd Ed.", Academic Press, 1990.

3. Fu K.S., "Syntactic Pattern Recognition", Prentice Hall, 1982.
4. Gonzalez R.C. and Thomason M.G., *Syntactic Pattern Recognition*, Addison-Wesley, 1978.
5. Chen C.H. Ed. "Proceeding of teh IEEE workship on expert system and Pattern Analysis world scientific", 1987.
6. K. Fukunaga, *Introduction to Statistical Pattern Recognition*, Academic Press, San Diego, California, USA, 1990.

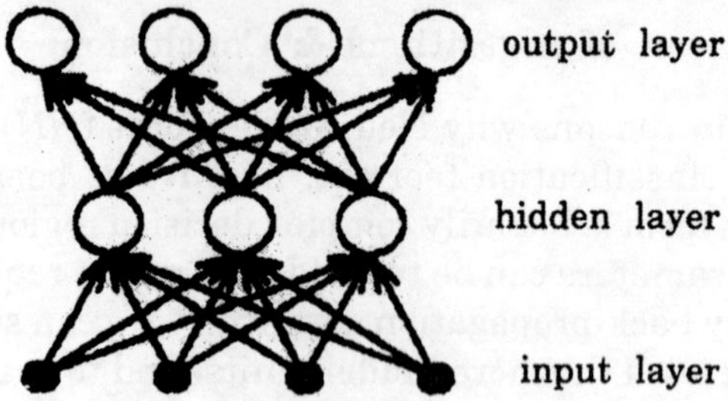

Figure 1: Multi layer perceptron with one hidden layer.

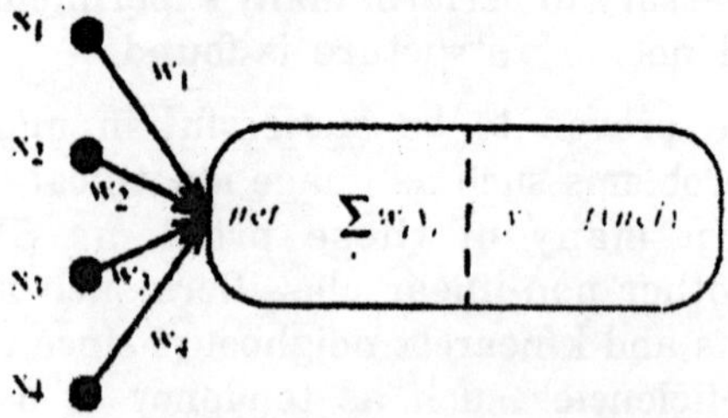

Figure 2: Basic processing unit

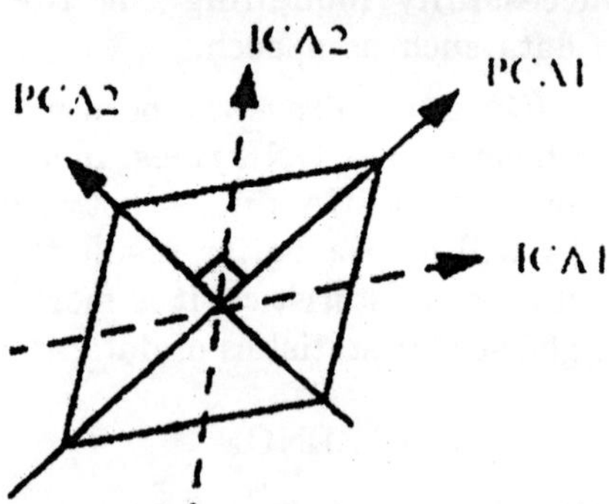

Figure 3: A comparison between transformations found by PCA and ICA when the data is uniformly distributed within the diamond-shaped region.

13

Fingerprint Matching

*Yashpal Singh**

*Priyank Tripathi***

Abstract

The Process for fingerprint image filter design, enhancement, matching with already present fingerprint images is studied. A new method of converting image to Gray-Value matrix and then matching it with other images is the focus of this paper. Image enhancement process includes smoothening, sharpening, contrasting and post-processing tasks. A flow chart shows the hierarchical steps taken in process of matching an originally scanned raw image to the final match.

Introduction

Fingerprints have been used as a positive human identifier for more than 100 years and along with palm and foot prints are still considered one of the most reliable means of distinguishing a man from his fellows. Although closely allied with the art criminal apprehension, human prints can and

*, ** Maithilisharan Gupt Bundelkhand Institute of Engineering & Technology Jhansi 284 001.

do provide unequalled methods of personal identification for various other areas, including intelligence and security, banking and credit, merchandising and drug abuse prevention. As a result of the need for foolproof and instantaneous verification of identity in these specialized convenient. Methods of evaluating human prints for identification has been greatly enhanced in recent years by the development of automated systems based on advancements in the topology of pattern recognition and data processing.

Finger Print Identification

Before the advent of automated systems, all finger prints were matched manually and visually, a slower method. Although, the aim of all automation in fingerprints is to produce a low-cost system that is fast, accurate and reliable. The ultimate decision regarding selection of equipment must be influenced by system equipment and user needs. It has been suggested that all user applications fall into one of the following categories:

- √ *Access Control*—Confirmation of identity to make a person gain access or entry to certain secure and classified area as soon as possible.
- √ *Transaction Control*—Same identification function as that of access control, but accompanied by search of a centralized database in order to provide both updated information and/or a means of further identification.
- √ *Production Processing*—It is mandatory to achieve high Identification rates with low false hit ratio, because of large number of fingerprint requests received in unit time.
- √ *Latent Print Processing*—Comparing one or more hopefully complete usually partial prints taken from the scene of crime against a special fingerprint database.

Fingerprints and Its Recognizers

Fingerprints are one of the best ways for the unique identification of a particular person. A schematic diagram shown in Fig. 1 briefly describes various steps taken by a recognizer.

A fingerprint image consists of narrow ridges separated by narrow background valleys. The real significance of finger pattern is mainly based on the following principles:

- √ *Unchangeability*—The configuration and details of the patterns are permanent and never change through the life until the skin disintegrates after death.
- √ *Uniqueness*—The degree of variation of the ridges is so high that two patterns with same characteristics never occur either in another figure of the same person or different individual.
- √ *Classification*—The fingerprint variations are within a limit, which allows a systematic classification of these configurations.

Extraction of Fingerprints & Its Enhancement

- *Extraction of Fingerprints*—Fingerprints are extracted by using a scanner and digitized to an image of 256 X 256 pixels of 32 gray levels.
- *Enhancement and Binarization*—The aim of enhancing fingerprint is to facilitate matching and classification process. The methods for enhancement range from simple, standard image processing technique for edge enhancement, two methods more similar to the one mentioned in this paper, the entailing matched, oriented filtering. Digitization at a different resolution requires redesign of filter mask size and coefficient values.

The fingerprint image may be corrupted by various kinds of noise causing breaks in the ridges, bridges between ridges, and overall gray-level intensity variation. Despite this noise, human can often analyze the image easily using such clues such as, local ridge orientation, ridge continuity, and small ridge curvature.

The digitized picture is enhanced to improve the quality by oriented filtering. The general approach to this is first, to determine local ridge orientations at each point in the image to produce orientation image. Second, to smoothen image and third, to apply matched oriented filters throughout the image. Finally post-processing is performed on the image to reduce background noise.

- *Fingerprint Filter Design*—The filter design procedure should be as automatic as possible to enable even a non-expert in filter design (or fingerprint analysis) to produce effective filters. Effective filters primarily entails increasing the contrast between foreground ridges and background valleys and reducing noise. Although, the original image is gray scale, we are interested in only two levels of information, the foreground ridges and the background valleys. The major stages of filter design are:
  1. The calculation of filter mask and other parameters.
  2. Determination of local ridge orientations throughout the image.
  3. Smoothening of the orientation image.
  4. Pixel-by-Pixel enhancement filtering of original image based on local ridge orientation, followed by binarization.
  5. Post-processing to reduce background noise.
- *Image Enhancement*—The main objective of enhancement is to process a given image so that the result is more suitable than the original image. Approach may be divided into two broad categories:
  1. Frequency Domain Method.
  2. Spatial Domain Method.

The Frequency Domain Methods are based on modifying the Fourier transform of an image. The Spatial Domain Method, on the other hand, refers to the image plane itself, and approaches in this category are based on direct manipulation of the pixel in an image.

Matching Implementation and Results

The procedure for matching fingerprints can be understood

by the flow chart shown in Fig. 2. Enhanced fingerprint image is convolved through the designed filter. Then, convolved image is matched with other convolved fingerprint image. When we subtract these images, the matrix values must be zero or at least, a sparse matrix, if both fingerprints are same.

Usually, this work is done in MATLAB language. There is a drawback, when we matched one fingerprint image with same image, but rotated at some angle, then they may not match meaning a false result.

We try to reduce these problems by rotating 1st fingerprint with constantly differing angles and other image also rotated with same angle, and then match it. Threshold value is used for matching the fingerprint image.

MATLAB does not support 3-D imaging otherwise; calculation of orientation of all fingerprints would have been a lot easier.

Scope for Future Work and Conclusion

We can classify fingerprints into 4 categories based on its characteristics—

1. Arch (Plain and Tented).
2. Loop (Radial and Lunar).
3. Whorl (Plain, Central Pocket, Double and Accidental).

Now, fingerprint images are stored in the database category wise. To match one fingerprint with given database, first this fingerprint is checked for the category of the image in the database. Then, this fingerprint is compared within the same category of the fingerprint database. By practicing this, numbers of comparisons are considerably reduced.

In the presented paper, matching technique of fingerprints is based on number of zeroes in the subtracted matrix of fingerprints that are to be matched. First, we calculate a threshold value, where threshold value is the maximum no. of zeroes in the matrix obtained by subtracting rotating two fingerprints at different angles. The other image (which is to be matched) is matched with the first. If resulting matrix has value equal or more than threshold value, prints are said to be matched.

Nowadays, there is an essential need of personal identification. The use of computer in the fingerprint matching process is highly desirable such as building security systems and the police work. Later, computers can also be used in simplifying the task of securing large file databases of fingerprints.

REFERENCES

1. Gonzalez R.C., *Digital Image Processing,* Addison-Wesley.
2. A Grasselli, On the Classification of Fingerprints-Some considerations of the linguistic interpretation of pictures, methodologies of pattern recognition, S. Watanabe, ed., pp. 253-273. Academic Press (1969).
3. V.V. Horvath, J.M. Holeman & C.Q. Lemond, Fingerprint Recognition by Holographic Technique, *Law Enforcement Science & Technology,* pp. 485-492, Academic Press (1967).
4. D.K. Isenor & S.G. Zaky, Fingerprint Identification using Graph Matching, *Pattern Recognition,* Vol. 19 No. 2, pp. 113-123, 1986.
5. Kameswara Rao & Kenneth Black, Type Classification of Fingerprints: A Syntactic Approach, *IEEE transaction on Pattern Analysis and Machine Intelligence,* Vol. 2, No. 3, May. 1980.
6. M. Kawagoe & A.Tojo, Fingerprint Classification, *Pattern Recognition,* Vol. 17, pp. 295-303, 1984.
7. C.K. Kingston, Problems in Semi-Automated Fingerprint Classification, *Law Enforcement Science & Technology,* Academic Press (1967).
8. Lawrence O. Gorman & Jeffrey V. Nickerson, An approach to fingerprint filter design, Pattern Recognition, 1989.

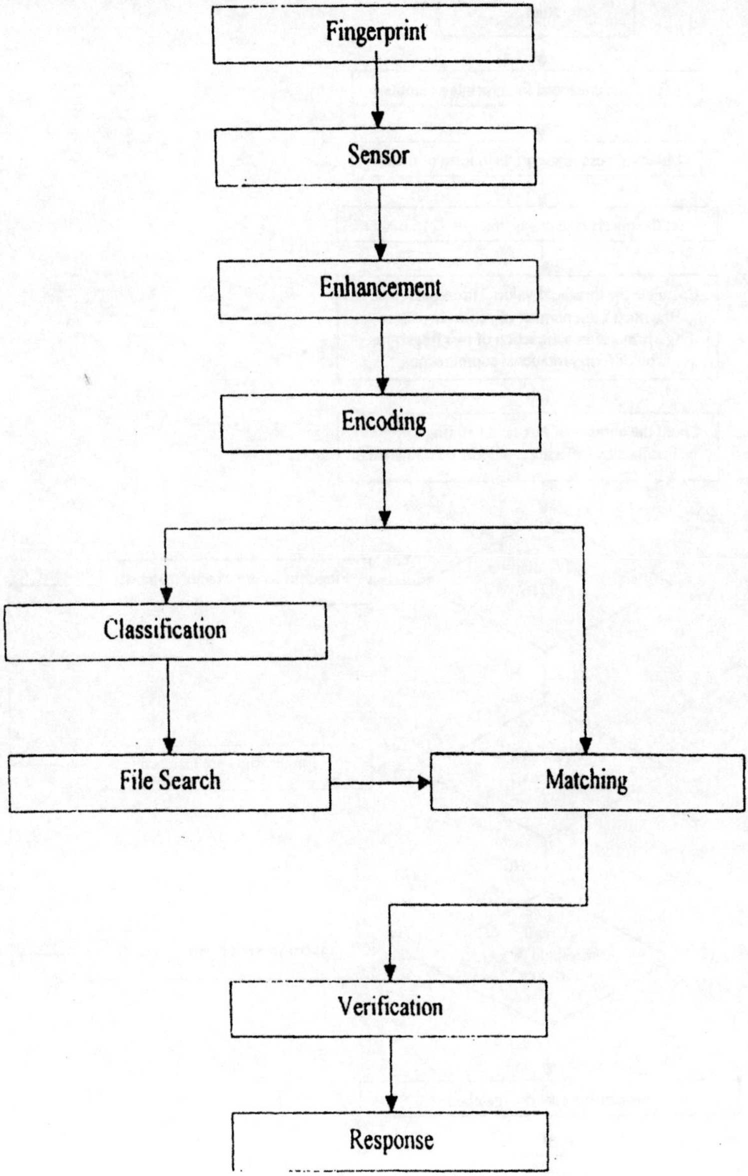

Figure 1: Steps Taken by A Pattern Recognizer

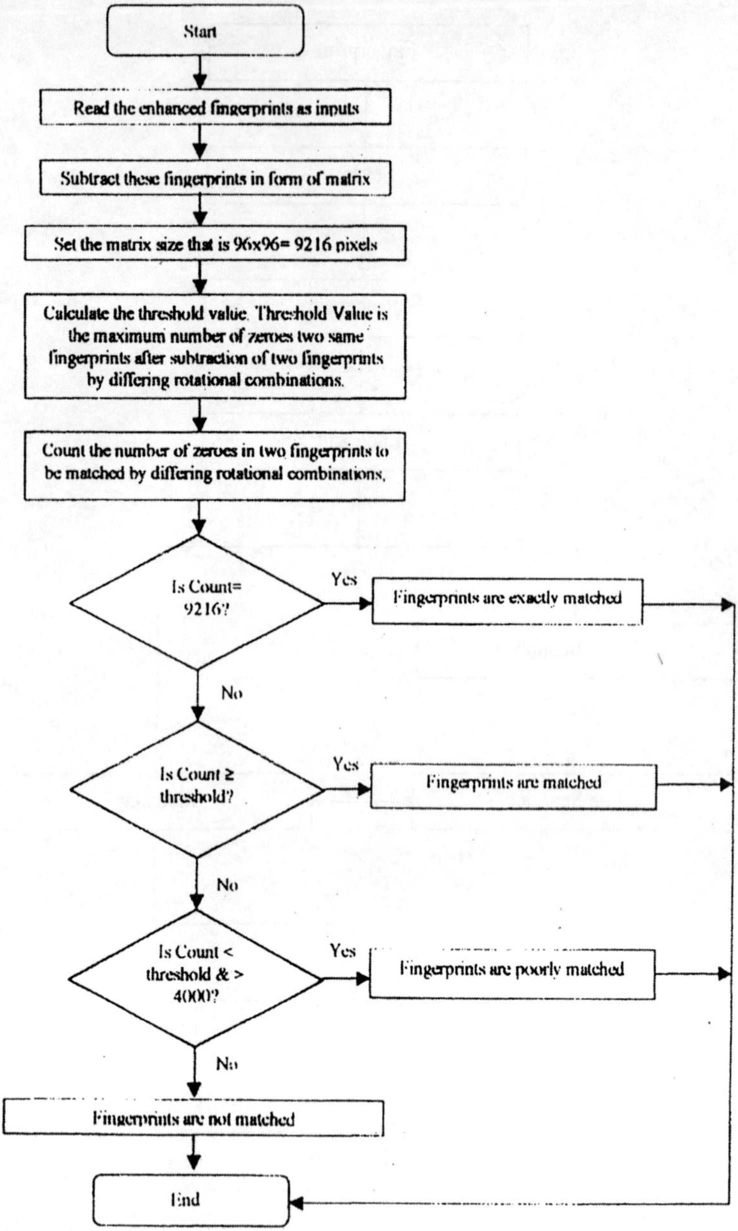

Figure 2: Flow Chart for Matching

14

Is Perfect Forgery Possible?

*S.K. Saxena**

It is the feeling and thinking of most of the persons that the science of handwriting identification is a weak science.

It is also presumed by them that the signature or writing of a person can be forged successfully.

It is also quoted so many times that there are persons in the market especially in the vicinity of the courts who can copy the signature or the writings of any person successfully.

This means that perfect forgery of a signature or writing is possible.

During the course of my 35 years of career in this profession I have not come across any such case of forgery where the expert could not detect it.

The reasons for the same are obvious which have been pointed out in the following paragraphs:

A simulated or copied or imitated forgery is a simulation or imitation of a genuine signature or writing.

A forgery of this class is produced by a method similar to that employed by a pupil in following a copy.

* G.E.Q.D. Kolkata.

Realisation of the fact that forgery is a criminal act, the fear of its discovery and the painful anxiety to do the work well, all combine to bring about a mental and muscular condition in the writer, that makes it very difficult if not altogether impossible to do the work in skilful manner.

For forgery one must be able to see the significant characteristics of the writings to be forged (another person).

And then must have the muscular skill necessary to reproduce them.

And at the same time eliminate all the characteristics of his own writings.

The result usually shows failure in all phases of the performance.

Simulation in almost every case gives attention to the conspicuous features of form only and the many other elements entering into the task receive no attention.

Natural writing is almost automatic act and follows the fixed grooves of habit but as soon as attention is given to it, it necessary becomes strained and unnatural.

If the imitator possesses skill superior to that of the writer of the writing imitated which in many cases is the fact the forgery many show a higher degree of muscular control than is exhibited in the genuine writing imitated.

The simulated signature and writing shows evidence of forgery as indicated by defective line quality, unnatural retouching, hesitated stroke condition, unusual pen lifts, interrupted and unnatural movements etc.

Further, as in the case of fingerprint identification it is a fact that fingerprints of two persons are not similar. Similarly in the case of handwriting identification, it is also certain that two persons can not write exactly alike.

Now if we take into consideration all the aforesaid statements, it is very reasonable to conclude that perfect forgery of a signature or writing is not possible.

15

History and Development of Fingerprints Identification System: A Review Paper

*P.K. Janjua;**
*N.K. Kanwal;***
*R.K. Garg;****
*Surender Nath*****

It is not exactly known as to who first used fingerprints for the purpose of identification and when. But the study of fingerprints and its uses can be traced back to the earliest forms of civilization. The use of fingerprints in the identification was started millions years ago and perhaps it is the oldest science.

The archaeologists are of the view that thousand of years before the birth of Christ, the fingerprints were being used on the pottery to mark its maker and brand markings.

Some scholars have referred to the impressions of fingerprints on the clay tablets for recording of business

*, **, *** Institute of Foresic Science & Criminology, Bundelkhand University, Jhansi 284 001.
****, Dept. of Anthropology Delhi Univesity, Delhi 110 007.

transactions in ancient Babylon and to the clay seals of ancient Chinese origin bearing thumb impressions.

The clay slabs with fingerprints nearly 3000 years old have been found in Tutankhamen's Tomb in Egypt. The fingerprints served as a seal to give authenticity to important documents in ancient Assyria.

Later thumbprints were used as official seal on documents by Chinese emperors since 240 B.C. These seals were made up of clays, which were bearing thumb impression and name of the owner on the other side. Emperor Ts-in-She (240-210 B.C) was the first imperial authority to use fingerprints seals in China and these Seals remained in use till the time of Emperor WU (187-156 B.C.).

The use of fingerprints seals very clearly express their significance for the purpose of Identification. Chinese documents of the Tong dynasty (618-906 A.D/) refer to fingerprints being impressed upon business contracts and this was continued in China up to 1278 A.D. during the Sung period.

The Spanish Pyrenees cave pictures, petroglyphics found on the Island of Garvin's off the northern coast of France, numerous rocks and paintings bearing hands designs and fingerprints shows that early man recognized the differences in the skin.

The work of Dr. Nehemiah Grew (1684) and Bidlo (1685) are among the earliest scientific descriptions of dermatoglyphics. He observed the patterns of the fingers and palms and described about the sweat pores and the arrangement of epidermal ridges. Bidlo in his book on Human Anatomy includes description of the arrangement of ridges in detail.

In 1686 Marcello Malpighi, Professor of Anatomy, University of Bologne (Italy) commented in his writing on the elevated ridges on the fingerprints.

It was during the 18th Century when many anatomical works appeared mentioning about the dermatoglyphics. Among them, the contributions of a German Scientist, Hintze (1747), Albinus (1764) were greatly appreciated and received more attention.

In 1770 an English wooden engraver and author, Thomas

Bewick used his own fingerprints for the purpose of ornamentation of his three books

Schroter (1814) while discussing the morphology of palmer skin explained the arrangement of ridges and pores.

Dr. Joannes Evangelista Purkinje, Professor of Anatomy University of Brestal have given a remarkable contribution in 1823, which is considered as an important landmark in the history of fingerprints science because he classified the varieties of fingerprint patterns systematically for the first time and mentioned them in his Latin thesis entitled "Commeantelio de Examines Physiologico Organ Vesusetc Systematic Cutaur" dated December, 22, 1823. He published a treatise commenting upon the diversity of ridge patterns on the tips of fingers, and further distinguished nine varieties of patterns of fingerprints. His work was intended only as a scholarly treatise and had no practical application to the problem of identification though he had hinted at some kind of probability of their utilization for the purpose of identification.

Sir William Herschel, I.C.S., Collector of Hoogly District (1858-1880) first made the official use of fingerprints for the purpose of Identification, when he first made a contractor to place his palm impressions on the contract, he did so to impress the man rather than as a mark of identification, In course of time, he discovered that finger impressions were individual and did not change with the passage of time. So he used fingerprints to prevent fraudulent collection of army pay accounts and also for the purpose of identity of other documents. He, however, did not formulate any classification formula.

Mr. Gabor, a photographer of San Francisco, accidentally noticed the lineation of prints in his inked fingerprints on a blotting paper and then he used them for the identification of Chinese laborers in 1880.

Dr. Henry Faulds, in 1880 wrote a comment on the practical use of fingerprints for the identification of criminals, while he was working at Tsukiji Hospital in Tokyo. His publication is the first item in the modern literature on the fingerprint identification. He further points out that chance print obtained from the scene of crime would provide positive identification of offenders when apprehended.

Sir Francis Galton (1888) utilized the materials and experience thus gained in his scientific study and established the individuality and permanency of fingerprints and devised the first scientific method of classifying fingerprints patterns. He proposed that fingerprints should be divided into three patterns i.e. whorls, loops and arches, due to this Galton system was adopted as supplement to the Bertillon's system. He published the book on fingerprints in 1892. The Home Office, London, officially recognized his work in 1894.

The need of the hour was to develop a classification system which should be adopted to file thousands of fingerprints in logical and searchable sequence. Dr. Jaun Vucetich, an Argentinean police officer fascinated by Galton's work devised a workable concept in 1891. His classification system has been refined over the years and still widely used in most Spanish-speaking countries.

Sir Edward Richard Henry (1891) Inspector General of Police of Lower Bengal subsequently started an extensive study in collaboration with two Indian Police Officers Khan Bahadur Azizul Haque, the Officer In-charge of the Anthropometric Bureau and Rai Bahadur Hem Chandra Bose of Bengal C.I.D., to develop a system of classifying the fingerprints. This system was proved so satisfactory in 1896 that an application was made to the Government of India for appointment of a committee to report upon the system. The committee consisting of Mr. C. Stratian, R.E., Surveyor General of India and Mr. Alex Pedler F.R.S. Principal, Presidency College, Calcutta examined both anthropometric system and Henry's system of classification of fingerprints and recommended for the adoption of fingerprints as a means of identification of the habitual criminals in place of anthropometric system in March, (1897) and due to explicitness of the method of classification this became very popular throughout the world as Henry Classification system.

On the 12th June 1897, by a resolution of the Governor General in Council, the system of identification through their finger impressions was adopted throughout India and the first fingerprints bureau in the world was officially established in Calcutta (India) in June 1897.

The use of fingerprints for the criminal identification was officially adopted in Scotland Yard, England and Wales during 1901. The systems of Henry and Vucetich form the basis of the modern Ten-digit fingerprint identification.

The FBI and law enforcement agencies throughout the United States used basic Henry system with some modifications and extensions.

Henry P. de Forset installed the first known systematic use of fingerprints in United States. New York States Prison at Albany ascribes the first systematic use of fingerprints in United States to identify criminals to Captain James Parke in 1903.

Leavenworth Penitentiary at Kansas together with St. Louis Police Department inaugurated fingerprint Bureaus in 1904, which were followed by the adoption of fingerprints system by US army in 1905, the U.S. Navy in 1907 and U.S. Marine Corps in 1908.

The use of fingerprints for the identification of criminals was officially adopted throughout the world during 1908 and thus overtook the application of Bertillion anthropometric card identification system.

In 1911-12, when Sir Edward Richard Henry, Commissioner, Metropolitan Police London, visited Calcutta and the officers of Bengal Police dined with him at the Bengal United Service Club, during this there was a presentation by Sir Edward Henry to the assembled company of his former Sub Inspector of Police, Khan Bahadur Azizual Haque as the man mainly responsible for the new worldwide fingerprint system of identification. After some 12 years the Government of India in recognition of his valuable service awarded this officer an Honorarium of Rs. 5,000.

In 1916 Rai Bahadur Hem Chandra Bose was the writer of a small handbook of Fingerprint Science, *Hints On Fingerprints.* He also developed a single print system and telegraphic code for transmission of fingerprints by telegraph.

In 1912 Monseuir Edmond Locard of Paris (France)

considered some other characteristics than that of Galton details and discovered that sweat pores on the ridges have individual shape and they are persistent throughout the life and their relative position on the ridges would also establish personal identity. His discovery is known as "Poroscopy".

Mr Chatterjee (1962), Director of Central Fingerprint Bureau, Govt. of India, Calcutta discovered that the edges of all ridges have special characteristics, which are also persistent throughout the life and therefore these are useful for personal identification. His discovery is known as "Edgeoscopy". Then he published his valuable paper in the *Fingerprint and Identification Magazine* published by the Institute of Applied Sciences; 1920 Sunnyside Avenue, Chicago, Ill., U.S.A. for the month of September, and distributed it throughout the world free of cost. He also suggested that personal identification could be made either from the Galton Details or from *Poroscopy or Edgeoscopy* singly or jointly. This combined method has been termed as *"Ridgeoscopy"* by Fingerprints Scientist D.R. Ashbaugh of R.C.M.P. Canada (C.f. Chatterjee and Hague; 1988).

The dermal palmer and plantar ridges are highly useful in biological studies. Their notably variable characteristics are not duplicated in other people, even in monozygotic twins or even in the impressions of different fingers of the same person. Because dermal ridges are found on a number of animals, it will be interesting to observe whether dermal patterns are replicated in cloning and if they vary how they vary. The details of these ridges are permanent. Yet while the individual characteristics are variable, that diversity falls within pattern limits that permit systematic classification (Cummins and Midlo; 1943).

It is evident from the seals found from Mohenjodaro and Harappa and our ancient books like *Ramayana* and *Mahabharata* were having the whole palm print known as 'Panja' which shows that fingerprints were used in the India since many centuries (Chatterjee; 1967). The patterns were first classified by Hindus in India as 'Shankh, and 'Chakra' etc.

As it is known that the primitive man were having the some knowledge about fingerprints but conversely it is little bit difficult to comment on when did the scientific study of fingerprints started.

Mayer (1788) made an attempt to explain about the some basic principles of fingerprints identifications. He explained that even though the arrangement of skin ridges unique but the there occurs the close similarity among some individuals and in spite of their peculiarities of arrangements all have a certain resemblances.

According to Forest (1974), the contributions of all four individuals were essential to the development of the fingerprint system as a means of personal identification. Faulds was the first to publish on the subject. Herschel was the first to establish a finger print system and to provide evidence for the persistence of the fingerprints over time. Henry improved the method of classification which resulted in its adoption by Scotland Yard. Galton's contribution was to bring together and strengthen the evidence that fingerprints could provide an ideal technique for personal identification.

Cummin and Midlo (1961) reported that in 1880, Tabor noticed the lineation of prints, which were accidentally made with his fingers on the blotting paper and carried out some experiments with his own fingerprints and proposed that the method of printing should be adopted for the registration of Chinese immigrants that went unheard.

Thompson (1882) used finger impression along with the signature for making payments to members of his party. Eber in 1888 presented the report to the ministry on practical usefulness of fingerprints, and the report went unheard (Heindl; 1929).

In 1930 Bettmann identified a minute characteristic as Island, which was earlier referred as an Enclosure. The island is small ridge, which is present between two disjoining segments and is having only one sweat pore. He was dealing with the terminology of fingerprints.

The various workers such as Wentworth (1918), Cummins

and Midlo (1961), Bridges (1963), Chatterjee (1967), Moenssons (1971), and Cowger (1983) worked for the improvements of methods of classification and identification from fingerprints and problems were sorted out for correct identification of patterns types and methods of comparison.

With the developments in the field of fingerprints science many other system were developed from time to time but could not get much fame due to passionate labour involved in them. Battely devised one such system in 1930 based on the classification of single digit fingerprint.

In 1960 Chatterjee, a fingerprints scientist from India invented a system of classification of Middle Phalanges Impressions fingers for use in dividing the heavy group 10 digits record. His paper was discussed at the general session of Interpol held at Madrid in 1960. He also invented a system of dividing the records of 10 Arches group, which was not possible so long (Chatterjee and Hague; 1988).

Dr. Jaun Vucetich established world's first fingerprints bureau in 1891, which still flourishes in La Plata, Argentina (Cooke; 1948).

Subsequently Federal Bureau of Investigation was established in 1924, which adopted Ten Digit Henry system of classification and established a fingerprint bureau and the fingerprints collected from the entire citizen were kept in this Bureau (F.B.I. 1941).

The problem of locating and maintaining the files of fingerprints arouses as with the passage of time the numbers of files of fingerprints increases to millions. This problem was sorted out with the introduction of computers developed Automated Fingerprint Identification System (Hazen, 1986).

The genetic points related with fingerprints have been studied by many workers and they reported that patterns types in monozygotic twins, twisting characteristics in elliptical whorls, twin loops and lateral pocket loops; ridge count or quantitative value of the pattern, breadth/height proportions and radial loops are all inherited characteristics (Galton, 1891,1892; Wilder, 1902; Bonnevie, 1924; Grunberg 1928; Penrose, 1954, 1965, 1972; Chattopadhyay, 1968, 1975; Penrose and Loesch, 1971 and Fraser et. al. 1986).

Even though efficient work have been done in the field of fingerprints concerned with various aspects of fingerprints but not much work is available on systematic study of the distribution of epidermal ridge minutiae and determination of sex of an individual from fingerprints.

The study of dermatoglyphic characteristics is very important, as during development the formation of epidermal ridges are effected by the maternal environment, gene deviants and chromosomal aberrations. Once formed pattern these are age and environment stable (Hootan, 1963).

The various fingerprint experts have studied the distribution of various epidermal ridge characteristics and methods developed in the past for quantitative assessment of fingerprints have been revised and found to be deficient (Stoney et. al., 1986,1987). The fingerprints comparison is sequential search for corresponding epidermal ridge minutiae in two fingerprints (Cowger, 1983). The distribution of epidermal ridge minutiae have been studied by few workers (Galton; 1892, Roxburgh; 1933, Amy; 1946; Santamaria, 1955; Kingston, 1964; Gupta; 1968, Okajima, 1970; Sclove, 1977; Dankmeije et. al., 1980; Banerjee and Sarkar, 1983; Stoney and Thornten, 1986).

Some fingerprints experts have given some points of consideration for determination of sex of an individual from fingerprint comparison during investigation of various types of cases, such as ridge breadth of fingerprints have specific value for females and males. Several workers have reported that the first trait likely to suggest itself for comparison in the sexes is ridge breadth. Ridges in the females are significantly finer (Cummins and Midlo, 1961). Adult women have epidermal ridge thickness of 0.40-0.50 mm while adult men have an epidermal ridge thickness of 0.50 mm (Cummins et al, 1941).

It has been reported that significant differences exist in the dermatoglyphic pattern of different tribes of town (Chai, 1971). He also considered sex variation in dermatoglyphics features as genetic in nature. Some other workers considered them physiological trait just as sex differences in stature and other physiological traits. A significant increase in whorls and decrease in loops patterns have been reported in some Indian population (Vishwanath and Vijaylakshmi, 1980).

Other fingerprints expert believes that women have finer epidermal ridge details (Moore, 1991) The studies conducted in the past regarding this hypothesis had suffered from small sample size or did not utilized empirical methods, which can determine its observed differences statistically significant within a race and gender (Cummins et al, 1941; Ohler, et al., 1983). In the recent past, for sex determination from fingerprints of an individual ridge density has been advocated as the most important parameter (Acree, 1999). The distributions of various fingerprints characteristics and its relationship with sex of an individual have been reported elsewhere (Janjua et. al. 2004).

BIBLIOGRAPHY

A. C. Bogle, T. Reed, and R. J. Rose (1994): Replication of Asymmetry of a-b Ridge Count and Behavioral Discordance in Monozygotic Twins, *Behavior Genetics,* 24 (1) Jan. 65-72.

Acree, M.A. (1999): Is there a gender differences in fingerprints ridge density, *Forensic Science International,* 102:35-41

Ahuja, V.R., Kant, K. and Tickoo, J.L. (1974): Genetic investigation among Khatri-Arora Punjabis of India. II. Dermatoglyphics. *Ind. J. Hered.,* 6: 13-18.

Ashbahgh, D.R. (1986): Poroscopy. *Identification,* Canada, 19 (1): 3.

Amy, L. (1946): *Valuer de la Preuve en Dactyloscopic de Paris,* 88:80-87

A. R. Hale (1951): Morphogenesis of volar skin in the human fetus. *Am. J. Anat* 91: 147-173.

Bade, W.F. (1934): Fingerprints on Pottery Aid In tracing Past, *Science News letter:* 261-262.

Balthazard, V. (1911): "De l' Identification par les Empreintes Digitales" Comptes Rendus des *Academies des Science,* Vol. 152: June; 1862-1864.

Bandopadhyay, K.K. and Dash Sharma, P. (1992): A topological approach to the finger dermatoglyphics of the Mundas of Kunti. *South Asian Anthro.,* 13 (1st and 2nd): 13-21.

Bandopadhyay, K.K. and Dash Sharma, P. (1995): A Study on the Finger Dermatoglyphics of the Asurs of Bihar. *Indian Anthropologist,* 25 (1): 31-38.

Banerjee, A.R. and Sarkar, N.C. (1983): Distribution of Epidermal ridge minutiae within the area of Finger patterns and Their significance in Identification, *Journal of Indian Academy of Forensic Sciences,* 22: 17-28.

Basu, A. (1971): Fingerprint patterns among three groups of Mysore Brahmins. *Man In India,* 51: 223-232.

Basu, A. (1983): Dermatoglyphics of the Muslim of Mysore city. *Hum. Sci.,* 32: 284-291.

Battley, H. (1930): *Single Finger Prints,* New Scotland Yard, H. M. Stationary Office.

Benham, William G. (1900): *The Laws of Scientific Hand Reading,* Knickerbocker Press, New York Health Research, Mokelumne Hill, CA reprint of the January, 1912 printing.

Bettmann, S. (1930): Zur Oberflachenmikroskepie der haunt am lebenden Menschen. *Arch. F. Dermat. U. Syph,* 161: 445-455.

Bhattacharjee, P.N. (1955): Dermatoglyphics of thc Abors of Assam. *The Anthropologist,* 2: 22-35.

Bidloo, G. (1685): *Anatomia Humani Corporis,* Amsterdam. Utrecht edition, *c.f.* Cummins, H. and Midlo, C. 1961: *Fingerprints, Palms and Soles.* Dover Publications, New York.

Biswas, P.C. (1957): Finger Dermatoglyphics of the Bhils of Rajasthan. The Anthropologist, 4: 2-4.

Biswas, P.C. (1961): Ethno-geographic variations in dermatoglyphics. *Proc. 2nd Inter Congress Human Genet.,* Rome, 1430-1449.

Bonnevie, K. (1924): Studies on Papillary patterns of human fingers. *J. Genetics,* 15:1-4.

Bridges, B.C. (1937): Personal Identification through the ages, *Fingerprint and Identification Maga., 19:51.*

Bridges, B.C. (1963): *Practical Fingerprints,* Funk and Wangnalls Company, New York.

Bridges, B.C. (2000): *Criminal Investigation, Practical Fingerprinting, Thumb Impression, Handwriting & Expert Testimony, Opinion Evidence,* The University Book Agency, 15 B Elgin Road, Allahabad.

Brown, W. (1946): Here we go again, *Fingerprint and Identification Mag.,* 28: 3-5.

Chai, C.K. (1971): Analysis of palm dermatoglyphics in Taiwan Indegeneous populations *American Journal of Physical Anthropology,* 34:369-376

Chatterjee, S.K. (1967): *Finger, Palms and Sole Prints,* Calcutta.

Chatterjee, S.K. and Hague, R.V. (1988): *Fingerprints or Dactyloscopy & Ridgeoscopy,* Kosa Publications, Calcutta.

Chattopadhyay, P.K. (1968): Genetic of the Dermal Ridges: Correlation between inter digital triradial distance in Palmer Dermatoglyphics. *Acta. Crim. Med. Legal. Japan,* 34: 163-167.

Chattopadhyay, P.K. and Dash Sharma, P. (1969): Finger Dermatoglyphics of the Karhi Brahmins of Bengal. *Am. J. Phys. Anthro.,* 30: 397-402.

Chattopadhyay, P.K. (1975): Causes of variation of the dermal ridges. *Jour. Ind. Acad. Forens. Sci.* Calcutta, 14:48-49.

Chattopadhyay, P.K. and Kushwaha, K.P.S. (1978): A Dermatoglyphic approach to the problem of Rajput Origins. *Mankind Quart.,* 18: 186-201 and 283-292.

Chattopadhyay, P.K. and Ganeson, D. (1984): Inheritance of Dermal Ridges : Relation between finger and palmer a-b Ridge Counts. *Jpn. J. Hum. Genet.,* 29: 59-61.

Cooke, T.D. (1948): World's first fingerprint bureau still flourishes in La Plata, Argentina, *Fingerprint Identi. Magazine;* 3-6.

Cowger, J.F. (1983): *Friction Ridge Skin,* Elsivier, New York: 151-189.

Cummins, H. (1930): The Fingerprints carvings of Stone-Age Men in Brittancy. *Sci. Monthly.,* 31: 273-279.

Cummins, H. (1941): Ancient fingerprints in Clay. *Sci. Monthly.,* 52: 389-402.

Cummins, H. and Midlo, C.(1961): Fingerprints palms and soles, *An Introduction to Dermatology,* p. 272.

Cummins, H.,Waits,W.J., M.C. Quitleg, J.T. (1941): The breadths of epidermal ridges on the fingerprints and palms, A study of Variation, *American Journal of Anatomy,* 68:129-150.

Dankmeijer, J. Waltman, J.M. and De Wilde, A.G. (1980): Biological Foundation for Forensic Identification Based on Fingerprints, *Acta Morphologica Netherlando-Scandivanica,* 18(1):67-83.

Dash Sharma, P (1978): Physical anthropological studies on Mundas, Oraons and Dushas of Bihar. *Field Research Project.* Miami, Florida, 1-84.

Douglas, F.H. and d' Harnoncourt, R. (1941): Indian Art of the United States. *The Museum of Modern Art,* New York.

de Forest, H.P. (1930): The evolution of the dactyloscopy in the United States, with an historical note on the first fingerprint bureau in the United States and a bibliography of personal identification.

Federal Bureau of Investigation (1941): *Classification of Fingerprints.* Washington Govt. Printing office.

Faulds, H. (1880): The Skin furrows of the hand. *Nature,* MacMillan and Co., London XXII: 605

Faulds, H. (1905): *Guide to Fingerprint Identification.* Wood, Mitchell and Co. Ltd. Hanley.

Fraser, F.C. and James, J. N. (1986): *Dermatoglyphics Genetics of Man,* Sec Ed. Lea and Febiger, Philadelphia.

Frederick Kuhne (1917): *The Fingerprint Instructor,* Munn & Company, Inc, New York,

Galton, F. (1891): Fingerprint indices. *Nature,* XLIV: 141.

Galton, F. (1892): Finger Prints, McMillan & Co. New Yorks; 100-103.

Ganeson, D. and Chattopadhyay, P.K., Sutherland, E. and Wolley, V. (1982): A Dermatoglyphic study of the Malays and Chinese of Malaysia, *Ann. Hum. Bio.,* 9: 283-285.

Ge, Liu Chun and Zhao Xiang Xin (1988): The Historical Application of Hand Prints in Chinese Litigation, *Jour. For. Ident.,* 38 (6) : 277-284.

Grunberg, H. (1928): Die Vererbung der menschlichen Tastfiguren. Zpschr.f.induct.abit u. *Vererbungslehre,* 50: 76-96.

Gupta, R., Janjua, P.K., Garg, R.K., Nath, S. (2004): The Distribution of Ridge Minutiae Among Baniya Community. (Communicated).

Gupta, S.R. (1968): "Statistical Survey of Ridge Characteristics," *International Criminal Police Review,* No. 218: 130-140.

Harris Hawthorne Wilder (1902): Palms and soles. *A,. J. Anat* 1:423-441;

Harris Hawthorne Wilder (1904): Racial differences in palm and sole configuration, *Am. Anthropologist,* 6:244-293;

Harris Hawthorne Wilder (1904): Duplicate Twins and double monsters (part only), *Am J. Anat.* 1904, 3:426-472;

Harris Hawthorne Wilder (1916): Palm and sole studies, *Biology Bulletin* 30:135-172, 211-252.

Harold Cummins and Charles Midlo (1926): Palmar and Plantar Epidermal Configurations (Dermatoglyphics) in Eurpoean Americans, *Am J Phys Anthropol,* 9:471-502

Harris Hawthorne Wilder, Inez Whipple-Wilder (1929): Revised methods of interpreting and formulating palmar dermatoglyphics, *Am J. Phys Anthropol,* 12:415-473.

Harold Cummins and Charles Midlo (1943): *Finger Prints, Palms and Soles An Introduction To Dermatoglyphics,* The Blakiston Company, Philadelphia.

Hazen, R.J. (1986): *Significant Advances in the Science of Fingerprints in Forensic Science,* 2 nd edition., G. Davies, Washington, D.C., American Chemical society

Heindl, R. (1929): Die erste deutsche Arbeit iiber das Fingerabdruckverfahren als polisciliches Identifiziercingmittel. *Arch. F. Kriminal.*, 85 : 30-69.

H. Faulds (1880): On the Skin furrows of the hand, *Nature* 22:605 (October 28, 1880)

Henry,E.R. (1900): Classification and Uses of Fingerprints, Routledge & Sons, London; 54-58.

Henry, E.R. and Gaensslen R.E. (1991): *Advances in Fingerprint Technology*—Elsevier, Science. Publishing Co., New York.

Henry, E.R. (1937): *Classification and uses of Fingerprints*—Eighth edition, H.M. Stationary office. London.

Herschel, W.J. (1894): Fingerprints. *Nature, LI-(77).*

Herschel, W.J. (1916): *The origin of fingerprinting,* London, Oxford University, Press.

Hootan, E.A. (1963): *Up From Ape.* The Macmillan Company, New York, p. 529.

Inez L. Whipple-Wilder (1904): The Ventral Surface of the Mammalian Chiridium *J. Morph Anthropol* 1904, 49:153-221.

Janjua, P.K., Garg, R.K. Nath, S., Kanwal, N.K. (2004): A Preliminary Study on The Distribution of fingerprint Characteristics and Its Relationship with Sex of Individual, *accepted for Oral Presentation,* 17th International Symposium, on Forensic Sciences, Wellington, NewZealand.

Jamshed Mavalwala (1978): *Dermatoglyphics, An International Perspective,* Moulton Publishers, The Hague - Paris, Aldine, Chicago, USA distributors..

Joannes Evangelista Purkinge, (1823): "Physiological Examination of the Visual Organ and of the Cutaneous System" *(Commentatio de Examine Physiologico Organi Visus et Systematis Cutanei)* Breslau: Vratisaviae Typis Universitatis, (Translated into English by Cummins, H, and R.W. Kennedy, *Am.J.Crim.Law.Criminol.* Vol. 31, pp. 343-356, 1940) .

Kaplysh, R., Janjua, P.K. and Garg, R.K. (2001): A Study On

Distribution of Fingerprints Patterns and Epidermal Minutiae, *Paper Presented, National Seminar On Recent Trends In Forensic Sciences,* University of Delhi, Delhi.

Kingston, C.R.(1964): Probabilistic Analysis of Partial Fingerprints patterns *D.Crim., Dissertation*, University Of California, Berkley: 37-38

Kothari, C.R. (1999): *Quantitative Techniques,* Vikas Publication House Pvt. Ltd., New Delhi.

Kristine Bonnevie (1924): Studies on papillary patterns of human fingers, *J Genet* 15:1-111.

Laufer, B. (1912): History of the Fingerprints System. *Ann. Report,* Smithsonian Inst. 631-652.

Laufer, B. (1917): *Concerning the History of the Fingerprints Science.* New York, The Science Press, 45: 504

Locard, E. (1912): Les pores at 1". Identification des criminals. *Biologica,* 2: 357-365.

Loesch, D.Z. (1971): Genetics of dermatoglyphic patterns on palms. *Ann. Hum. Genet.* London. 34: 277-293.

Malpighi, M. (1686): *De Extreno Tactus Organo.* London.

Mayer, J.C.A. (1788): Anatomische Kupfertafeln nebst dasu gchorigen Erklarungen (fingerprints described in the last section).

Midlo, C. (1934): Form of hand and foot in primates. *Am. J. Phys. Anthropo.* XIX (3)

Midlo, C. and Cummins, H. (1931): Dermatoglyphics in Eskimos *Am. J. Phys. Anthropo.* XVI (1).

Moore, R.T. (1991): Automatic fingerprints identification system in H.C. Lee R.E. Gaenstles (Eds) *Advances in fingerprints technology,* CRC Press ISCOAETON, 1969.

Nath, S. (1984): *Fingerprints Identification,* Geeta Press, C-7 Bhajanpura, Delhi.

Noel Jaquin (1934): *The Hand of Man,* Faber & Faber Ltd, London.

Noel Jaquin (1940): *The Signature of Time,* Faber & Faber, Ltd., London.

Noel Jaquin (1942): *The Hand Speaks Your Health, Your Sex, Your Life,* Lindoe & Fisher, London.

Norris M. Durham and Chris C. Plato (1990): *Trends in Dermatoglyphic Research,* Kluwer Academic Publishers: Dordrecht/Boston/London.

Okajima, M. (1970): Frequency of Forks in Epidermal Ridge Minutiae in the fingerprint. *Amer. Jour. Phys. Anthro.,* Vol-32,: 100-113.

Ohler, E.A. and Cummins, H. (1992): Sexual differences in breadth of epidermal ridges on the fingertips & palms, American Journal of Physical Anthropology, 29: 341-363.

Panwar, A., Janjua, P.K. (2004): A Preliminary Study on The Fingerprints of Jats of Haryana *(Communicated).*

Penrose, L.S. (1954): The distal tri-radius on the hands of parents and sibs of Mongols in Imbeciles. *Ann. Hum. Genet.* London, 19: 10.

Penrose, L.S. (1965): On the geometry of loops and deltas. *Ann. Hum. Genet.* London, 29: 207-211.

Penrose, L.S. (1969): Dermatoglyphics. *Scient. Am.* 72-84

Penrose, L.S. and Loesch, D. (1971): Dermatoglyphic patterns and clinical diagnosis by discriminant functions. *Ann. Hum. Genet.* London. 35: 51-60.

Plato, C.C., Cereghino, J.J. and Steinberg, F.S. (1975): The Dermatoglyphics of American Caucasians, *Amer. Jour. Phys. Anthro.,*: 42: 195-210

Roxeburgh, T. (1933): "On the Evidential Value of Finger Prints," Sankhya: *Indian Journal of Statistics,* Vol. 1.: 189-214.

Santamaria, F. (1955): A New method for evaluation of ridge characteristics, *Fingerprints and Identification Magazine,* 36 (11):3-18.

Schroter, J.F. (1814): Das nenschliche Gefiihl oder organ des Getastes. Leipzig.

Sclove, S.L. (1977): The Occurrence of Fingerprint Characteristics as a Two-Dimensional Poisson Process," *Journal of The American Statical Association.* No.1.74, No. 367: p. 594

Stoney, D.A. and Thornton, J.I. (1986): A Critical Analysis of Quantitative fingerprints Individuality model, *Journal of Forensic Sciences,* 31(4):1187-1216.

Stoney, D.A. and Thornton, J.I. (1987): A systematic study of epidermal ridge minutiae, *Journal of Forensic Science, 32:1182*-1203

United States Department of Justice, Federal Bureau of Investigation (1917): *The Science of Fingerprints, Classifications and Uses,* (Rev. 12-84) U.S.G.P.O., pp. 11-18 especially, see also for example:

Viswanathan, C.P. and Vijaylakshmi, G. (1980): Sex dimorphism and handedness in dermatoglyphics in south Indian Population, *Journal of Anatomical Society of India,* 29 (2): 87-90

William J. Babler (1990): *Prenatal Communalities in Epidermal Ridge Development, pp. 54-68 in Trends in Dermatoglyphic Research,* edited by Norris M. Durham and Chris C. Plato, Kluwer Academic Publishers, Dordrecht/London/Boston .Vol 1, *Studies in Human Biology.*

W. Hirsch and J. U. Schweichel (1973): Morphological evidence concerning the problem of skin ridge formation. *J. Ment. Defic. Res.,* 17:58.

16

A Study on Eruption of Third Molar of the Jat Sikhs and Muslims of Punjab

*A. Singla**
*P.K Janjua***
*N.K. Kanwal****

Introduction

It is often necessary to position an individual accurately upon a particular time scale. Such information is commonly required to assist in the establishment of identity but may be helpful in legal cases concerned with the age of the individuals (Harvey, 1974). Age determination from teeth, in case of living, may be required in sports participation, marriage, adoption and inheritance of property, etc. While in case of the dead the problem may arise in the identification of individuals in cases of mass-disasters, accidents, human right violations, etc. The age of an adult individual can be determined by using various parameters. Among these parameters dental features are the most important since, they are least affected by environmental

*, **, *** Institute of Forensic Science & Criminology, B.U. Jhansi-284128.

conditions after the death of an individual. Several scientists tried to estimate the age of an individual from teeth. Krogman (1948) summarized the seven stages of dental eruption from birth described by Hellman (1932) while Nolla (1964) observed ten stages of dental development. Since 1950, age determination techniques from the tooth took a different direction. Gustafson in (1950) had emphasized on the changes on an anterior tooth for the assessment of age. He used 6 methods namely attrition, periodontosis, secondary dentine, cementum apposition, root resorption, transparency of the root. Third molars, often called 'The wisdom teeth', are always of special interest. They are used for the estimation of age of an individual widely; the range of age of eruption is in between 17 to 25 years in most cases. Because of this wide range of eruption of third molar, Survey Committee (1964) suggested to the Govt. of India for zonewise detail study of the problem of determination of age from third molars. The time of eruption of third molar is more uncertain. The third molar has wide range of population variation in their emergence, is known to exist (Fanning, 1962). Eruption times of each of the teeth were found to vary not only from population to population but also within the same population. A number of factors such as improved nutrition (Dahlberg and Maunsback, 1948), Social Class, Urban living condition, growth in body size, skeletal and sexual maturation, marked changes in environment (Clements et. al, 1953; Billewicz et. al, 1975) were found to influence the eruption time and sequence of eruption of permanent teeth. All third molars, mandibular and maxillary, show more variations in development than any other teeth in the mouth (Ash, 1984). In the present study an attempt has been made to determine the age of eruption of the third molars, and their variation in two communities namely, the Muslims and the Jat-Sikhs of the Panjab.

Human Dentition: Function

Dentition refers to the various kind of teeth generally arranged on the jaws inside the buccal cavity of organism. These are primarily meant for the cutting, crushing and grinding food. In addition, these may be used as organ of offense and defense.

Though, teeth are found in diverse groups of vertebrates, yet they are highly specialized in man. Their main function in man is to chew and prepare food for swallowing.

Structure of Teeth

Teeth is a calcified papilli of the skin secondary implanted in the bones of the jaws as subserving the function of mastication. Each tooth consists of three parts:

1. The *Crown,* projecting beyond the gum,
2. The *Root,* embedded in the alveolus of the maxilla or the mandible,
3. The *Neck,* which is the constricted part between the crown and the root.

Each tooth in man is composed of three calcified tissues. *Enamel, Dentine* and *Cement* and one delicate specialized connective tissue, the *pulp.* The dentine forms the bulk of the tooth, but normally it is not exposed on the surface of the tooth. It is covered in one region by the enamel and in another by the cement. The pulp cavity is situated in the middle, which contains the pulp tissue, surrounded by the dentine, which forms the boundaries of pulp cavity. At the apex of each root there is a small foramen in the cement and dentine through which blood vessels and nerves pass into the pulp. Each tooth is implanted in a socket which is formed by the alveolar bone of the upper or lower jaw. The part of the tooth, implanted in the bone is root area and it is attached to the alveolar bone by the periodontal membrane.

Teeth As An Evidence of Evolution

In the course of the evolution of the vertebrates many modifications of the teeth have appeared. From paleontological records it is evident that homodont type of dentition was the first to arise, where all the teeth were alike i.e. peg shaped and which later on got differentiated into the various kinds of teeth thus giving rise to heterodont type of dentition, in which the teeth are differentiated into incisors, canines, premolars and molars as in mammals. In mammals this differentiation of the teeth can be regarded as an adaptive division of labour. The incisors acting as cutting or chisels, the canines as daggers, and the molars, usually with many cusps as grinders. Thereafter, from Eutherian stage the Heterodont type of dentition reduction in the number of teeth took place to give the present day dental formula of 2.1.2.3/2.1.2.3 from 3.1.4.3/3.1.4.3. Along with the reduction in number of teeth, reduction in the size and shape also occurred, the size of various teeth like incisors and canines remained either unchanged or reduced to small sizes respectively on account of their masticatory habits. The jaw size also changed along with this. Premolars get reduced in number as well as went under molarization. The molars have also undergone certain changes in their cusp pattern from tri-tubercular stage to multi-tubercular stage. (Scott & Symon, 1977).

Review of Literature

According to Survey Committee Report (1964) on Medical College Practice in India, determination of age of an individual is a necessity for the law enforcement agencies in both civil and criminal matters. Survey Committee, has recommended to the government of India to encourage Zone-wise study of the problem of determination of age. As the standard books gave, the age of eruption of third molar is between 17 to 25 years, but Survey Committee suggested that this wide range of 8 years is not much useful, when accurate assessment of age is required in Medico-legal cases.

Several workers have attempted to determine the age from eruption sequence of teeth in various populations (Cohen, 1928; Dahlberg and Maunsback, 1948; Mackay and Martin, 1952; Clements *et.* al., 1953; Dahlberg and Menegaz - Bock, 1958; Nanda 1960; Barrett, Brown and Cellier, 1964). Fanning (1962) examined 3423 white high school and college students (2370 males and 1053 females) between 13 to 22 years of age for the third molar emergence in mutilated and non-mutilated dentition. No statistically significant difference was found between the emergence of left and right third molars in either maxilla or mandible. The mandibular third molars erupts earlier than the maxillary. Similar type of observations were also made by Billewicz and McGregor (1975) but with the exception of premolars. Whereas, Nolla (1964) studied the development of the teeth using X-rays of 25 males and 25 female and has observed that dental development starts early and complete earlier in females as compared to males. He also observed 10 stages of development of teth. Whereas Nayak and Patel (1977) and Sidhu and Gupta (1973); examined the sequence and eruption time of permanent teeth among the Tibetans and the Punjabis of Patiala, respectively, varying in age from 5 to 23 years. They observed bilateral variations in eruption times both in the upper and lower jaw of the males andfurther observed the earlier eruption of the mandibular teeth as compared to the maxillary teeth in males with the exception of first premolar. Singh (1978, 1980a) studied the eruption of permanent dentition in the case of Gaddi Rajputs of age varying from 4 to 20 years of the Dhula Dhar Range of the Himalayas and observed that the bilateral difference and upper and lower jaw differences in the eruption ages are non-significant. Hassanali (1985) obtained data on the third molar eruption from a cross-sectional study of 1343 African and 1092 Asian school and University students aged 13-23 years. Africans were significantly ahead of Asians in the third molar emergence. In Africans, the median eruption age for the third molar teeth in the lower jaw was 17.95 years (right) and 18.24 years (left) and in upper jaw it was 18.76 years (right) and 18.89 years (left). The corresponding ages in Asians in the lower jaw were 19.97 years (right) and 19.89 years (left) and in the upper jaw were 20.65 years for both right and left. Whereas, Ajmani et al. (1986) carried out a study in an attempt to estimate the eruption age of wisdom teeth (third molar) in the North Nigerian population of 654 boys and 584 girls ranging in age from 11-23 years. In general, teeth of the lower jaw erupted earlier than those of the upper jaw and teeth of left side erupted earlier than the teeth of right side. The wisdom tooth erupted a little earlier amongst male (18 years) as compared with female (18.5 years). In 1998, Singh, Z. studied frequency distribution of eruption of third molar (M3) and also taken into account the sequence of eruption of both right and left sided mandibular and maxillary teeth in Jat-Sikh males of age group between 5 to 20 years. He found that mandibular teeth erupted earlier than the maxillary teeth except premolars and also showed that the third molar tooth erupted late during the age of 20th year. He also observed the bilateral difference in the eruption of third molar. Pathak et al. (1999) examined 100 males and 74 females radiologically from Jaipur age ranging from 13 to 25 years. In this study an attempt was made to estimate age by developmental stages of third molar teeth. The development of third molar teeth was divided into 10 developmental stages. Socio-economic status and religion has no effect on the eruption and development of various stages of third molar teeth.

Materials and Methods

The present work has been carried out to study the age of eruption of third molar in people belonging to *Jat-Sikh* and *Muslim* communities of Panjab. The age of the subjects ranged from 16-25years.

Jat Sikh

The *Jats* are one of the agricultural communities distributed all over Panjab, U.P. Delhi, and Rajasthan. They are known from the 8th century A.D. forming a considerable portion of *Sind* together with the *Meds* as 'wild people plundering on the roads' (Sen, 1963).

Their rebellions against the *Arabs* caused punitive expeditions. Consequently, it is not surprising to find a section of them in Baluchistan today converted to *Islam*. They were always in arms against Islamic invaders. They sometimes founded coalitions with kindred tribes and rose against the foreign rulers. There exists a variety of views regarding their origin.

1. They are considered as 'outsiders' who came in different waves of migration to India.
2. An opposing view is that they are considered as an indigenous people who had their homeland in southeast Punjab near Delhi (Field, 1959).

3. Chattopadhyay, however, raised the opinion that they originally were *Rajput* who fell in social status due to their adoption of widow marriage. Jat Sikhs are endogamous but practice *gotra* (clan-like organization) exogamy.

Muslims

Muslim is an Arabic word that means "one who surrenders himself to God". They are follower of Islam, Islam arises is Arabia in the 7th. century A.D. as a result of the preaching and teaching of the Prophet Muhammad. Islam is a major religion of world. It began in Arabia and spread to all parts of the world. Around A.D. 570, when *Muhammad* was born, the influence of both *Judaism* and *Christianity* was experienced in Arabia. With the founding of the *'ummah'*, the Muslim community, in the autumn of 622, the Islamic era begins. Reliable census figures are not available. Yet there are 600, 000, 000 Muslims in the world today, the majority are *Sunnis*. The historicists came to be known as *Sunnites,* their main opponents, as *Shi'ites.* Each group relied on the *Sunnah,* but emphasized different elements. For the *Sunnites,* who should more properly be called the Jamai-Sunnites, the principle of Solidarity was essential to the *Sunnah.* The Shi'ites argued that the fundamental element of the Sunnah, and one will fully overlooked by the Jama'I-Sunnites, was Muhammad's devotion to his family and his wish that they succeed him through' Ali. In India, they are considered as outsiders. Muslim marry within their own community and the marriages are usually 'arranged'. Thus they form an endogamous group.

The study was conducted in various schools, colleges, localities and villages in and around Malerkotla and Patiala cities of the Panjab. The study was conducted on 527 Muslim (236 males and 291 females) and 631 Jat-Sikh (281 males and 350 females) between 16 to 25 years of age. All the subjects were apparently healthy looking and belonged to mixed socio-economic strata. The subjects of the study were divided into following groups between age.16-17 years, 17-18 years, 18-19 years, 19-20 years, 20-21 years, 21-22 years, 22-23 years, 23-24 years, 24-25 years, 25 years and above

The Name, Age, Sex, Caste, Economic status, Nutritional status, Disease, if any and other relevant information were also recorded. Each and every subject was examined to study the third molars in the upper and lower jaws. Each subject was questioned to determine the status of the missing third molar, which may have been extracted or never erupted at all. The presence or absence of one or more third molar was then recorded. A tooth was considered to have erupted only, when a portion of the crown of the tooth, however very small, may be, had penetrated the gingival. Thus, gingival emergence was used as the criteria for eruption. Comparison for presence or absence of the third molar in the two communities and in the males and females of a community have been made by the chi2 (÷2) test using the G-tables (Singh and Bhasin, 1989). The probability values have been determined by referring to Fisher Table (Fisher, 1953).

Results and Discussions

The results of eruption of third molar in case of males and females of both the Jat-Sikh and Muslim communities of Punjab are given in table 1 and 2. It is evident from the table 1 that at the age of 16 years, no third molar was erupted at all. At the age of 17 years, no maxillary third molar had been erupted except in Muslim females (11.1 %), but at the age of 18 years females of both the communities show the eruption of right and left maxillary third molar. The eruption of mandibular third molar started at the age of 17 years in males and females of both the communities. The percentage of eruption of right and left mandibular third molar is more as compared to maxillary third molar (table 1 & 2). It is evident from the table 2 that Jat Sikh males shows maximum percentage of eruption frequencies (90.9%) of mandibular third molar at the age of 23 years. While, Jat Sikh females show maximum percentage of eruption (82.4%) at the age of 25 years. On the other hand, Muslim males show the maximum percentage of eruption (95.8 %) at the age of 21 years and Muslim females show the maximum percentage of eruption (85.3%) at the age of 25 years.

Thus, it is clear from the table 1 and 2 that eruption frequency was not 100% neither in males nor in females at both the communities, in any age group.

Comparison for the presence or absence of third molars between the two sexes among the Jat Sikhs and the Muslims; and between the Muslims and Jat Sikhs have been made and the Chi2 *(x2)* value are given in table 3 to 6. It is evident from table 3 and 4 that the differences between the two communities are statistically insignificant, but the sex difference in the Muslims is statistically significant (Table 5), while, it is insignificant between males and females of Jat Sikh (Table 6).

The present study shows that dental development and eruption starts early in females than males which is in accordance observations made by Nolla (1964). But it differs from the study of Ajmani et. al. (1986) according to which wisdom tooth erupted a little earlier amongst males as compared with females.

According to the present study, the mandibular third molars erupts earlier than the maxillary. It is in accordance with the observations made by Fanning (1962); Sidhu and Gupta (1973); Billewicz and Mc Gregor (1975); Nayak and Patel (1977); Ajmani et. al. (1986) and Singh (1998).

In the present study, bilateral variations were observed in the eruption times of mandibular and maxillary third molars. The result obtained are in accordance with Sidhu and Gupta (1973); Nayak and Patel (1977); Singh (1978, 1980a), Ajmani et. al. (1986);Singh (1998), but are contrary to Fanning (1962); Billewicz and McGregor (1975).

Table 1: Frequency of Eruption of Third Molar (M3) in Various Age Groups In Parentheses % age is given

		MALE					FEMALE				
Age	Community	No. of subjects	Maxillary		Mandibular		No. of Subjects	Maxillary		Mandibular	
			Right	Left	Right	Left		Right	Left	Right	Left
16 years	Jat-Sikh	21	-	-	-	-	20	-	-	-	-
	Muslim	21	-	-	-	-	19	-	-	-	-
17 years	Jat-Sikh	25	-	-	3 (12%)	1 (4%)	25	-	-	5 (20%)	4 (16%)
	Muslim	23	-	-	1 (4.34%)	2 (8.6%)	18	-	2 (11.1 %)	4 (22.2%)	6 (33.3%)
18 years	Jat-Sikh	25	-	-	2 (8%)	-	30	5 (16.6%)	5 (16.6%)	7 (23.3%)	9 (30%)
	Muslim	22	-	-	3 (13.6%)	2 (9%)	22	1 (4.5%)	4 (18.1 %)	10 (45.4%)	13 (59.0%)
19 years	Jat-Sikh	25	4 (16%)	4 (16%)	9 (36%)	10 (40%)	27	13 (48.1%)	11 (40.7%)	13 (48.1%)	13 (48.1 %)
	Muslim	23	. 9 (39.1 %)	9 (39.1 %)	10 (43.4%)	11 (47.8%)	20	2 (10%)	4 (20%)	11 (55%)	8 (40%)
20 years	Jat-Sikh	25	5 (20%)	6 (24%)	10 (40%)	7 (28%)	20	12 (60%)	12 (60%)	16 (80%)	15 (75%)
	Muslim	24	6 (25%)	6 (25%)	11 (45.8%)	9 (37.5%)	22	5 (22.7%)	5 (22.7%)	9 (40.9%)	10 (45.4%)

Table 2: Frequency of Eruption oF Third Molar (M3) In Various Age Groups
In Parentheses % age is given

		MALE					FEMALE				
Age	Community	No. of subjects	Maxillary		Mandibular		No. of Subjects	Maxillary		Mandibular	
			Right	Left	Right	Left		Right	Left	Right	Left
21 years	Jat-Sikh	25	13 (52%)	15 (60%)	17 (68%)	16 (64%)	29	17 (58.6%)	17 (58.6%)	20 (68.9%)	19 (65.5%)
	Muslim	24	21 (87.5%)	22 (91.6%)	22 (91.6%)	23 (95.8%)	21	11 (52.3%)	11 (52.3%)	14 (66.6%)	16 (76.1%)
22 years	Jat-Sikh	23	15 (65.2%)	17 (73.9%)	18 (75.2%)	17 (73.9%)	24	18 (75%)	18 (75%)	19 (79.1 %)	18 (75%)
	Muslim	20	15 (75%)	15 (75%)	16 (80%)	16 (80%)	18	14 (77.7%)	13 (72.2%)	16 (88.8%)	15, (83.3 %)
23 years	Jat-Sikh	22 (68.1 %)	15 (77.2%)	17 (90.9%)	20 (90.9%)	20	20 (58.3%)	14 (54.1 %)	13 (75%)	18 (79.1%)	19
	Muslim	20	16 (80%)	15 (75%)	16 (80%)	16 (80%)	18	15 (83.3%)	15 (83.3%)	15 (83.3%)	15 (83.3 %)
24 years	Jat-Sikh	23 (69.5%)	16 (69.5%)	16 (78.2%)	18 (86.9%)	20	20 (7C%)	14 (75%)	15 (75%)	15 (75%)	15
	Muslim	17	13 (76.4%)	13 (76.4%) \	13 (76.4%)	14 (82.3%)	17	14 (82.3%)	14 (82.3%)	15 (88.2%)	14 (82.3 %)
25 years +	Jat-Sikh	67 (71.6%)	48 (79.1 %)	53 (85%)	57 (82%)	55	131 (82.4%)	108 (82.4%)	108 (82.4%)	108 (82.4%)	108
	Muslim	42	37 (88%)	36 (85.7%)	37 (88%)	37 (88%)	116	98 (84.4%)	98 (84.4%)	99 (85.3%)	99 (85.3 %)

Table 3
Comparison Among the Jat-Sikh Males and Muslim Males

Third Molar	*No. of Muslim Males*	*No. of Jat-Sikh Males*	*Total*
Absent	89	94	183
Present	126	166	292
Total	215	260	475

Chi² (X^2)= 1.364 Probability (P) =.30> P> .20
Significant/Insignificant= Insignificant

Table 4
Comparison among the Jat-Sikh Females and Muslim Females

Third Molar	*No. of Muslim Females*	*No. of Jat-Sikh Females*	*Total*
Absent	64	95	159
Present	208	235	443
Total	272	330	602

Chi² (X^2)= 2.133 Probability (P) =.20>P>.10
Significant/InSignificant=Insignificant

Table 5
Comparison Among the Muslim Males and Females

Third Molar	*No. of Muslim Males*	*No. of Muslim Females*	*Total*
Absent	89	64	153
Present	126	208	334
Total	215	272	487

Chi² (X^2)= 17.755 Probability (P)=.001 > P
Significant/Insignificant= Significant.

Table 6
Comparison Among the Jat-Sikh Males and Females

Third Molar	*No. of Jat-Sikh Males*	*No. of Jat-Sikh Females*	*Total*
Absent	94	95	189
Present	166	235	401
Total	260	320	590

Chi² (X^2) =3.613 Probability (P)= .10>P>.05
Significant/Insignificant= InSignificant

Summary

1. Below 17 years there is no eruption of third molars in males and females of Jat-Sikhs and Muslims.
2. Mandibular third molars show earlier eruption and greater percentage of eruption in the both the sexes of both the communities.
3. Both Muslim and Jat-Sikh females show earlier eruption of third molar than Muslim and Jat-Sikh males respectively.
4. For presence or absence of third molar, the differences between the two communities are statistically insignificant.
5. Sex differences in Muslims are statistically significant, while it is insignificant between Jat-Sikhs.
6. Even after the age of 25 years, there are lots of cases where third molar had not erupted at all.

REFERENCES

Ajmani, M.L., Jain, S.P., and Joshi, S.D. (1986). Age and Wisdom teeth in Nigeria. *Anthrop. Anz.,* 44 : 143-148.

Ash, M.M. (1984). *Wheeler's Dental Anatomy, Physiology and occlusion, VI. Ed. W.B. Saunders Compo Philadelphia.* pp. 243- 275.

Barrett, M.J., Brown, T. and cellier, K.M. (1964). Tooth eruption sequence in a tribe of Central Australian Aborigines. Am. J. *Phys. Anthrop.* 22: 79-90.

Billewicz, W.Z., and Mc Gregor, I.A., (1975). Eruption of Permanent teeth in West African (Gambian) children in relation to, age, sex and physique. *Ann. Hum. Biol.,* 2 : 117-128.

Chattopadhyay, P.K. (1969). A genetic study of Jats of Delhi and the Panjab, *Ph.D. Thesis,* University of Delhi.

Clements, E.N.B., Thomas, E.D. and Picket, K.G. (1953). Time of Eruption of permanent teeth in Bristol children in 1947, 48, *Br. Med. J.,* 1: 1421-1424.

Cohen, J.T. (1928). The dates of Eruption of the permanent teeth in a group of Minneapolis children: A preliminary report. *J.* Am. *Dent. Asso.,* 15 : 2337-2341.

Dahlberg, A. A. and Menegaz - Bock, R.M. (1958). Emergence of the permanent teeth in Pima Indian Children: A critical analysis of method and an estimate of population parameter. *J. Dent. Res.,* 37: 1123-1140.

Dahlberg, G. and Maunsback, A.B. (1948). The eruption of the permanent teeth in the normal population of Sweden. *Acta. Genet.,* 1 : 77-91.

Fanning, E.A. (1962). Third Molar emergence in Bostonians. *Am. J.Phys. An throp 01.* 20 : 339-345.

Field, H. (1959). *An Anthropological reconnaissance in West Pakistan,* Paper of the Peabody Museum, Vol. 52.

Fisher, R.A., (1953) : *Statistical Methods for Research workers* Oliver and Boyd, Ltd. Edinburg.

Gustafson, G., (1950). Age determination on teeth. *J. Amer Dent. Assn,* 41 : 45-54.

Hassanali, J. (1985). The third permanent Molar eruption in Kenyan Africans and Asians. *Ann. Hum. Biol.,* 12: 517-523.

Harvey, W. (1974). The Estimation of age from the Dentition. *J. Forens. Sci. - Soc.,* 14: 215-221.

Krogman, W.M. (1948). The Contributions of Milo Hellman, D.D.S., to Physical Anthropology. *Am. J. Orthod,* 43(1) : 61

Mackay, D.H. and Martin, W.J. (1952). Dentition and Physique of Bantu Children. *J. Trop. Med. Hyg.,* 55: 265-275.

Nanda, R.S. (1960). Eruption of human teeth. *Am. J. Orthod.,* 46: 363-378.

Nayak, S.K. and Patel, S. (1977). Age of Eruption of permanent teeth and its sequence among the Tibetan Refuges. *J. Indian Med. Assoc.,* 69 : 146-149.

Nolla, C.M. (1964). The development of the permanent teeth *J. Dent. Child.* 27, 254.

Pathak, et al. (1999). A study of Eruption of Third Molar in Relation To Estimation of Age In People of 13 to 25 years Age group. *JFMT Vol.* 16, 17-19.

Scott, J. H. and Symon, N. B. B. (1977). *Introduction to dental anatomy,* Eighth Edition, Churchill Livingstone. London and New York. pp-416-422.

Sen, A.K. 1963. *Peoples and Polities in Early Mediaeval India* (1206-1398 A.D.), India Book Distributing Co., Calcutta. pp. 134-136.

Sidhu, L.S. and Gupta, P. (1973). Sequence and age of eruption of permanent teeth in the Punjabi population of Patiala. *The Eastern Anthropologist,* 26: 261-270.

Singh, S.P. (1978). Growth Patterns from 4 to 20 years of Male Rajput Gaddis—A Himalayan Tribe. *Ph.D. Thesis (unpublished),* Punjabi University, Patiala.

Singh, S.P. (1980a). Eruption of permanent teeth in Gaddi Rajput males of Dhaula Dhar Range of Himalayas. *J. Morphol. Anthropol.,* 70: 295-301.

Singh, I.P. and Bhasin, M.K. (1989). *A Laboratory Manual on Biological Anthropology.* 222-227.

Singh, Z. (1998). Development Age In Jat-Sikh Boys from 5 to 20 with special Reference to skeletal, sexual and Dental Maturity. *Ph.D. Thesis (Unpublished)* Punjabi University, Patiala.

Survey Committee (1964) *Report on Med. College Practice in India,* Director General of Health Sciences, Ministry of Health, New Delhi, P. 63.

17

Prediction of Stature through Hand and Foot Lengths Among Brahmins of Himachal Pradesh

*Surinder Nath**
*Divya Chugh***
*Renu Rani****
*Bhavna*****

Introduction

Examination of skeletal remains is important in the process of establishing identity of the deceased, as it involves assessment of age, sex, ethnic group, ante mortem stature while determination of stature from the skeletal remains has somehow attracted attention of researchers from various disciplines and a considerable number of studies have been conducted all over the world in this regard. In India, researchers have formulated both regression formulae as well as Multiplication Factors (MFs) on available skeletal populations as well as on the living population groups (Athwale, 1963; Patel et al., 1964; Joshi et al., 1964; 1965; Kolte and Bansal, 1974; Duggal and

*, **, ***, ****, (Department of Anthropology, University of Delhi, Delhi-110007)

Nath, 1986; Nath et al., 1988; 1990; Nath and Krishan, 1990; Anand and Nath, 1990; Nath et al., 1991; Nath and Routray, 1996; Nath, 1997; Kaur and Nath, 1997; Jain and Nath, 1997; Nath and Kaur, 1998; Nath et al., 1999). Most of these studies pertain to estimation of stature from long limb bones of different living Indian population groups. These studies further reflect that the long limb bones exhibit a moderate to high correlation with stature.

It is a well known fact that the long bones of the lower limb have a higher value of correlation with stature than the one observed with the long bones of the upper limb as the lower limb bones contribute directly to the stature of a person while the upper limb bones do not. But we do use the upper limb bones for this purpose as in certain cases one may come across only upper limb bones. It has also been observed that certain other body parts besides long bones also exhibit moderate to high correlation with stature as observed with long limb bones. Nath (1997) reported the use of hand and foot lengths for estimation of stature on the premise that both these lengths exhibit significant relationship with stature (correlation value above 0.05).

In the present study an attempt has been made to formulate regression formulae for estimation of stature from hand and foot lengths among male and female Brahmins of Sundernagar Tehsil, District Mandi, Himachal Pradesh.

Sundernagar is situated at a height of 1000 meters above the mean sea level on Kiratpur Sahib-Kullu National Highway Number 21.The Tehsil of Sundernagar is inhabited by Rajputs, Brahmins, Khatris, Kanets and scheduled castes like Lohar, Koli, Jogi, Julahe, Gujjars etc. However, the Rajputs and the Brahmins are dominant caste groups of Sundernagar Tehsil.

Material and Methods

Data for the present study comprises of 200 Brahmins (95 males and 105 females) belonging to Sundernagar Tehsil. All the subject ranged in age from 17 to 20 years and were measured for hand length (HL), foot length (FL) and stature (S) in accordance with the standard measurement techniques (Martin and Saller (1959) and Nath (1993).

Stature (S): It is obtained as a projective distance from the standing surface to the highest point on the head (vertex) in the standard standing position, using anthropometric rod.

Hand Length (HL): It is obtained as a distance between the proximal bracelet crease and the distal most of the middle finger (Dactyl ion) when the left hand is fully stretched with finger together and palm facing upwards, using sliding caliper.

Foot Length (FL): It is obtained as a distance between the most distal point on the tip of the longest toe (Acropodion) and the most posterior point on the heel of the foot (Pternion) when the foot is fully stretched with entire weight on the left foot, using rod compass.

Data were subjected to statistical analysis to obtain measures of central tendency and dispersion for assessing sex differences in these measurements. Subsequently, correlation coefficient was calculated for assessing the relationship between stature and hand and foot lengths for formulation of sex specific regression formulae for prediction of stature using SPSS programme.

Results and Discussion

Preliminary analyses reveal that the male Brahmins are not only taller than their female counterparts but they also have longer hands and feet (Table-1). The apparent differences observed in the mean values of all the three body dimensions reveal highly significant sex differences ($p<0.01$).

Owing to highly significant sex differences data have been treated separately for correlation analysis and formulation of regression formulae for prediction of stature among Brahmins of Sundernagar.

Table – 2 exhibits correlation coefficient values between hand and foot lengths and stature for both male and female Brahmins along with their respective regression formulae for prediction of stature. It is evident from the table that foot length exhibits higher correlation with stature for both male (r=0.823) and female (r=0.467) Brahmins as compared to hand length (r=0.792 for males and r=0.389 for females). It is also observed that both hand and foot lengths have sufficiently greater value of correlation among males ((value of r above 0.79) in contrast to their female counterparts (value of r between 0.389 and 0.467, which is less than 0.05) who show only a moderate relationship with stature. The standard error of estimate (SEE), which is an important indicator of a reliable estimate of stature, is somewhat on the higher side for both male and female Brahmins on using hand and foot lengths in contrast to the one observed with long limb bone lengths. However, the SEE is sufficiently low when such an estimate is obtained using lengths of femur or tibia (lower limb long bones).

Table-3 lists thirty-six regression equations, formulated for prediction of stature from hand length, including sixteen male, nineteen female and one male and female combined living population groups of India, to provide a comparative view of the association between hand length and stature in different Indian populations.

It is evident from the table that the value of correlation between hand length and stature varies from a minimum of 0.274 to a maximum of 0.943. It is further observed that twenty-eight regression equations exhibit a value of correlation above 0.5 among which nine equations show the correlation value beyond 0.7.

Indicating that hand length could be used as an important indicator for prediction of stature for both male and female groups. The other important indicator of reliability of such an estimate is the standard error of estimate. It is evident from the table that the value of SEE is not listed for seven out of thirty-six regression equations. The value SEE varies from a minimum of +1.49 to a maximum of +11.57.The reliability of such an estimate is dependent over the error of estimate as the low value of SEE suggests greater reliability in the estimated stature and in this table only three population exhibit SEE value less than +3.0 while eighteen equations exhibits its value above +5.0. However both male and female Brahmins of Sundernagar show a relatively high value of SEE indicating that hand length should be used to estimate stature with great caution.

Table-4 presents thirty-five regression equations (fourteen male and twenty-one female) formulated for prediction of stature from foot length for different living population groups of India to provide a comparative of relationship between foot length and stature in different living population groups.

A close examination of the table reveals that the value of correlation coefficient ranges from a minimum of 0.213 to 0.921. It is further observed that twenty-seven regression equations exhibit this value above 0.5, out of which eleven equations have this value beyond 0.7 and only one equation has this value above 0.9, indicating that foot length could be used for estimation of stature with reasonable accuracy. However, the standard error of estimate is available only for twenty-nine out of thirty five regression equations and it ranges between a minimum of +1,66 and a maximum of +9.50. It is observed that the value of SEE is less than +3.0 for only three out of twenty-nine equations while fifteen equations exhibit this value above +5.0 suggesting that foot length could be used as an indicator for estimating stature in general, despite the fact that both male and female Brahmins exhibit the value of SEE on the higher side suggesting that it may not provide as accurate estimates of stature as obtained on using femur of tibia. But in the absence of long bones like femur or tibia it could be used to have an approximation of stature.

It may thus be emphasized here that out of the two body measures, the hand length and foot length, considered in the present study, foot length would provide a relatively better prediction of stature as it exhibits a high correlation with stature and a relatively low standard error of estimate than the hand length among both male and female Brahmins.

It is also noticed that the male Brahmins exhibit relatively higher correlation value between stature and the lengths of hand and foot than the female Brahmins but the males also exhibit low standard error of estimate than the females for both the dimensions thereby suggesting that the accuracy in the predicted stature would be greater among on using foot length than the hand length as compared to the female Brahmins.

Table 1
Sex Differences in Stature, Hand and Foot Lengths among Brahmins of Himachal Pradesh

		Male		*Female*		*Value of t*
S.No.	*Body Dimension*	*Mean (cm)*	*S.E x*	*Mean (cm)*	*S.E X*	
1.	Stature	159.96	1.09	152.86	0.52	5.86*
2.	Hand Length	16.13	0.10	15.58	0.07	5.98*
3.	Foot Length	24.97	0.14	22.81	0.09	12.80*

* Significant at 1% level ($p<0.01$)

Table-2
Regression Formulae for prediction of Stature among Male and Female Brahmins of Himachal Pradesh

S.No.	*Sex*	*Regression Formulae*	*SEE*	*Value of r*
1.	Male	-3.94 + 6.56 (FL)	8.75	0.823
2.	Male	17.24 + 8.75 (HL)	10.42	0.792
3.	Female	93.56 + 2.60 (FL)	8.80	0.467
4.	Female	109.50 + 2.80 (HL)	10.50	0.389

Table 3
Regression Equations for Prediction of Stature through Hand length Among different Living Indian Population Groups

S.No.	Population/Sex/Area	Author/Year	Regression Equation	SEE	Value of r
1.	Punjabi (M) Patiala	Bhatnagar et al.1984	127.97 + 2.06 HL	-	-
2.	Brahmin (M) Ranikhet	Tiwary 1986	106.01 + 2.99 HL	5.79	0.560
3.	Rajput (M) Ranikhet	Tiwary 1986	44.05 + 6.58 HL	5.42	0.830
4.	Brahmin (M) Garhwal	Anand 1990	80.38 + 4.64 HL	-	0.618
5.	Brahmin (F) Garhwal	Anand 1990	44.59 + 6.42 HL	-	0.943
6.	Brahmin (M) Garhwal	Anand 1990	149.03 + 0.89 HL	-	0.299
7.	Brahmin (F) Garhwal	Anand 1990	83.39 + 4.16 HL	-	0.587
8.	Hindu Baniya (F) Delhi	Nath & Krishan 1990.	68.89 + 4.96 HL	5.40	0.679
9.	Punjabi (F) Delhi	Nath et al. 1990	85.22 + 4.05 HL	5.43	0.594
10.	Mongoloid Type (M+F), Mainpur	Momonchand 1992	125.5 0+ 2.00 HL	7.00	-
11.	Jat (M) Churu, Rajasthan	Rautray 1995	37.90 + 6.98 HL	-	0.863
12.	Rajput (M) Himachal	Kaur 1996	96.74 + 3.83 HL	-	0.480
13.	Rajput (F) Himachal	Kaur 1996	80.39 + 4.38 HL	-	0.660
14.	Sikh (M) Delhi	Kaur 1998	89.13 + 4.31 HL	4.57	0.599
15.	Sikh (F) Delhi	Kaur 1998	88.64 + 4.04 HL	3.99	0.639
16.	Brahmins (M) Garhwal	Nath et al. 1998	104.41 + 3.46 HL	8.53	0.585
17.	Brahmins (F) Garhwal	Nath et al. 1998	101.19 + 3.14 HL	8.39	0.536
18.	Rajputs (M) Garhwal	Nath et al. 1998	123.22 + 2.37 HL	11.57	0.345
19.	Rajputs (F) Garhwal	Nath et al. 1998	96.27 + 3.56 HL	9.31	0.597
20.	Bengali Badiyas (F)Delhi	Nath et al. 1998	137.17 + 1.03 HL	4.37	0.274
21.	Bengali Sudras (F) Delhi	Nath et al. 1998	58.31 + 5.67 HL	2.18	0.865
22.	Punjabi (F) Delhi	Sethi 1998	87.85 + 3.92 HL	6.46	0.596
23.	Jain (F) Delhi	Sethi 1998	66.73 + 5.15 HL	8.29	0.627
24.	Jain (M) Delhi	Jain 1999	86.35 + 4.34 HL	4.44	0.624
25.	Jain (F) Delhi	Jain 1999	89.50 + 3.80 HL	4.26	0.556
26.	Jat (F) Delhi	Jain et al.1999	108.54 + 2.95 HL	5.01	0.440
27.	Brahmins (M) Kumaon	Kaur et al.1999	76.56 + 4.82 HL	8.43	0.661
28.	Warli (M) Maharastra	Kaur et al.1999	78.47 + 4.49 HL	7.59	0.739
29.	Bengali Kayasthas (F) Delhi	Nath et al. 1999	60.66 + 5.54 HL	2.36	0.830
30.	Bengali Brahmins (F) Delhi	Nath et al. 1999	63.97 + 5.42 HL	1.49	0.904
31.	Meiteis (M) Mainpur	Sunita Devi 2001	84.47 + 4.42 HL	4.48	0.620
32.	Meiteis (F) Mainpur	Sunita Devi 2001	74.51 + 4.65 HL	3.92	0.661
33.	Rajput (M) Sundernagar	Nath et al. 2002	4.45 + 9.48 HL	10.52	0.756
34.	Rajput (F) Sundernagar	Nath et al. 2002	82.90 + 4.52 HL	9.67	0.582
35.	Brahmin (M) Sundernagar	Nath &Chugh,2002	17.24 + 8.75 HL	10.42	0.792
36.	Brahmin (F) Sundernagar	Nath &Chugh,2002	109.50 + 2.80 HL	10.50	0.389

Table 4
Regression Equations for Prediction of Stature through Foot length Among different Living Indian Population Groups

S.No.	Population/Sex/Area	Author/Year	Regression Equation	SEE	Value of r
1.	Adult (M) Chandigarh	Qumera et al.1980	75.45 + 3.64 FL	4.34	0.690
2.	Adult (F) Chandigarh	Qumera et al.1980	75.41 + 3.43 FL	4.02	0.700
3.	Brahmin (M) Ranikhet	Tiwary 1986	114.91+ 2.04 FL	6.39	0.450
4.	Rajput (F) Ranikhet	Tiwari 1986	37.19 + 5.71 FL	7.20	0.700
5.	Brahmin (M) Garhwal	Anand 1990	114.97+2.01 FL	-	0.425
6.	Brahmin (F) Garhwal	Anand 1990	64.30 + 3.93 FL	-	0.921
7.	Rajput (M) Garhwal	Anand& Nath 1990	126.65+ 1.58 FL	-	0.213
8.	Rajput (F) Garhwal	Anand& Nath 1990	101.90+ 2.30 FL	-	0.448
9.	Hindu Baniya (F) Delhi	Nath &Krishan 1990	57.27 + 4.13 FL	5.09	0.746
10.	Punjabi (F) Delhi	Nath et al. 1990	84.65 + 2.99 FL	4.74	0.642
11.	Rajput (M) Sirmour	Nath & Kaur 1998	69.74 + 3.82 FL	-	0.660
12.	Rajput (F) Sirmour	Nath & Kaur 1998	71.70 + 3.62 FL	-	0.698
13.	Sikh (M) Delhi	Kaur 1998	79.73 + 3.51 FL	4.23	0.671
14.	Sikh (F) Delhi	Kaur 1998	78.73 + 3.40 FL	3.73	0.696
15.	Brahmins (M) Garhwal	Nath et al. 1998	103,31+ 2.52 FL	7.84	0.624
16.	Brahmins (F) Garhwal	Nath et al. 1998	105.91+ 2.06 FL	8.45	0.497
17.	Rajputs (M) Garhwal	Nath et al. 1998	117.50+ 1.94 FL	9.50	0.452
18.	Rajputs (F) Garhwal	Nath et al. 1998	98.17 + 2.47 FL	7.33	0.676
19.	Bengali Badiyas (F) Delhi	Nath et al. 1998	92.88 + 2.71 FL	3.59	0.613
20.	Bengali Sudras (F) Delhi	Nath et al. 1998	64.55 + 3.78 FL	1.99	0.889
21.	Punjabi (F) Delhi	Sethi 1998	88.04 + 2.95 FL	5.55	0.652
22.	Jain (F) Delhi	Sethi 1998	76.06 + 3.46 FL	7.01	0.648
23.	Jain (M) Delhi	Jain 1999	88.34 + 3.10 FL	4.30	0.588
24.	Jain (F) Delhi	Jain 1999	90.03 + 2.80 FL	4.14	0.668
25.	Jat (F) Delhi	Jain et al.1999	84.23 + 3.05 FL	4.38	0.621
26.	Brahmins (M) Kumaon	Kaur et al.1999	82.08 + 3.24 FL	9.47	0.591
27.	Warli (M) Maharastra	Kaur et al.1999	71.69 + 3.49 FL	8.84	0.715
28.	Bengali Kayasthas (F) Delhi	Nath et al. 1999	75.16 + 3.41 FL	2.21	0.853
29.	Bengali Brahmins (F) Delhi	Nath et al. 1999	53.52 + 4.38 FL	1.66	0.880
30.	Meiteis (M) Mainpur	Sunita Devi 2001	92.24 + 2.97 FL	3.73	0.650
31.	Meiteis (F) Mainpur	Sunita Devi 2001	70.02 + 3.72 FL	3.61	0.711
32.	Rajput (M) Sundernagar	Nath et al. 2001	11.74 + 6.02 FL	9.48	0.844
33.	Rajput (F) Sundernagar	Nath et al.2001	104.15+2.17 FL	8.76	0.482
34.	Brahmin (M) Sundernagar	Nath & Chugh, 2002	-3.94 + 6.56 FL	8.75	0.823
35.	Brahmin (F) Sundernagar	Nath & Chugh, 2002	93.56 + 2.60 FL	8.80	0.467

REFERENCES

Anand, N. and Nath, S. Estimation of Stature through percutaneous measures of upper and lower extremities among Rajputs of Pauri Garhwal. *Ind. J. For.Sci.* 5: 83-89 (1990).

Athwale, M.C. Estimation of height from lengths of forearm bones: A case study of one hundred Maharashtrians male adults of age between 25 and 30 years.*Am.J.Phys.Anthrop.* 21: 105-121(1963).

Duggal, N, and Nath, S. Estimation of Stature using percutaneous lengths of radius, ulna and tibia among Lodhas and Mundas of district Midnapore W. Bengal. *Anthropologie.* 24: 23-27(1986)

Jain, P. and Nath, S. Estimation of stature through upper and lower limb dimensions among Brahmins of Kumaon. *Ind. J. Phy. Anthrop. & Hum. Genet.* 20: 163-168(1997)

Joshi, N.B., Patel, M.P. and Dongre, A.V. Regression equation of height on ulnar length. *Ind. J. Med. Res.* 52: 1087-1091(1964)

Joshi, N.B. Patel, M.P. Amin, M.C. and Dongre, A.V. Use of tibia and ulna in estimating total body height. *Ind.J.med.Res.* 53: 831-834(1965).

Kaur, S. and Nath, S. Reconstruction of stature from various dimensions of upper extremity among Sikh females of Delhi. *Procs.Xth All India Forensic Science Conference, Bhubaneswar (11-13th Nov.1997):* 6-16(1997).

Kolte, P.M. and Bansal, P.C. determination of regression formulae for reconstruction of stature from long bones of upper limb in Maharashtrians of Marathwadaregion. *J. Anat. Soc. India.*23: 6-11(1974).

Martin, R. and Saller, K. *Lehrbuch der Anthropologie in Systematicher.* Fisher Darstellung.Stuttgart. (1959).

Nath, S. *Anthropometry: The Measurement of Body Size, Shape and Form.* Friends Publication India, Delhi. (1993).

Nath, S. Estimation of stature through hand and foot lengths among Jats of Rajasthan. *Police Research and Development Journal.* Qr.IV: 20-22. (1997).

Nath, S., Duggal, N. and Chandra, N.S. Reconstruction of stature on the basis of percutaneous lengths of forearm bones among Mundas of Midnapore district, W.Bengal. *Human Science.* 37: 170-175(1988).

Nath, S., Rajni and Chhibber, S. Reconstruction of stature from percutaneous lengths of upper and lower extremity segments among Punjabi females of Delhi. *Ind.J. For.Sci.* 4: 171-181(1990).

Nath, S. and Krishan, G. Determination of stature using percutaneous measurements of upper and lower limbs among Hindu (Baniya) females of Delhi. *J.Anthrop.Soc. India.* 39; 151-166 (1990).

Nath, S. and Rautray, N. Estimation of stature from different bone dimensions of upper limb among Jats of Churu, Rajasthan. *The Ind.J. Criminal. and Criminalistics.* 17: 85-91(1996).

Nath, S., Kaur, S., Jain, P. and Joshi, P.C. Reconstruction of stature among Rajputs and Brahmins of Srinagar, Garhwal (U.P.) *South Asian Anthropologist.* 20: 63-66(1999)

Patel, M.P., Joshi, N.B. and Dongre, A.V. Regression equation of height and tibial length. *Ind.J.Med.Res.* 52: 531-534(1964).

18

Formulation of Multiplication Factors for Estimation of Stature Using Upper Extremity Dimensions Among Male and Female Tangkhul Nagas of Manipur

*L. Sunita Devi**
*Surinder Nath***

Introduction

Forensic anthropology, an applied discipline, is a branch of physical anthropology, which interacts with other disciplines pertaining to the understanding of crime and its investigation. Examinations of long limb bones recovered from a scene of crime, have often been used by the forensic anthropologists to extract relevant information about the victim. One such aspect pertains to reconstruction of living stature from such skeletal remains. Numerous researchers have proved beyond doubt, through their studies, that such means of stature reconstruction are both population and sex specific as the

*, ** Department of Anthropology, University of Delhi, Delhi-110007.

body proportions differ significantly from one population to another as well as from one sex to the other.

In India, perhaps due to non-availability of the skeletal remains, as different ethnic groups have their own traditions for disposal of death bodies, we come across a different situation and we do not have well-documented skeletal populations, which could be used to formulate means of stature reconstruction. Thus, in the absence of a well documented skeletal collection researchers have focused their attention towards living population groups and have obtained relevant measurements of the bone lengths over the skin and correlated them with the living stature to obtain the degree of relationship of these bone lengths exhibit with stature. Based on these correlation values linear regression equations have been formulated for different Indian population groups treated separately for both the sexes.

Keeping the relationship of the long limb bones with stature in mind an attempt has been made in the present study to reconstruct stature among male and female Tangkhul Nagas of Manipur using four body measurements pertaining to upper extremity dimensions.

Material and Methods

Data for the present study comprises of 203 Tangkhul Nagas (104 males and 99 females) inhabiting the Ukhrul district of Manipur.

Tangkhul Nagas are one of the original inhabitants of Manipur state in the North Eastern part of India, who are largely found in Ukhrul district along with some Kuki tribes and few Nepalese. Very few of them inhabit in other districts of Manipur such as Chandel, Thoubal and Senapati. According to 2001 Census, the total population of Tangkhul Nagas is estimated as 1,25,000. They are purely mongoloid group who have epicanthic eye fold, fair complexion, long faces, black and smooth hair, prominent checks and short to medium stature. However, few tall persons are also seen. They speak their own dialect, which belongs to Tibeto-Burman language family. Each and every Tangkhul village has its own language but they communicate through their common dialect.

Tangkhul Nagas are Christian by religion adopted since 1896. Before that they were animists. They are agriculturalist and practice shifting, terrace and ploughing cultivation. Thus, agriculture is the main source of income and weaving, carpentry, cottage industry, animal husbandry, farming, government services and business are other occupations, which are secondary source of income. Rice is the main staple food for them. They are very much fond of non-vegetarian food. "Zalm" (local rice beer) is a part of their food item. But after Christianity they stopped taking wine except some elderly people and youngsters. Few old women also consume local liquor. They also love simple boiled vegetable foods. They wear both traditional and western cloths.

All the subjects ranged in age from 20 to 40 years were measured for the following four measures of upper extremity, i.e., upper arm length (UAL), radial length (RL), ulnar length (UL) and hand length, besides stature following the standard measurement techniques recommended by Martin and Saller, 1959, Allbrook, 1961 and Nath, 1993.

Description of Measurements

1. Stature (S): It is obtained as a projective distance between standing surface (floor) and the vertex, the highest point on the head in mid-sagittal plane, when the subject is standing in the standard position, using anthropometer rod.
2. *Upper arm length (UAL):* It is obtained as a direct distance between the left acromion and the lower end of the lateral epicondyle of humerus, using rod compass.
3. *Radial length (RL):* The left acromion is flexed and semipronated with the hand in natural position. It is obtained as a distance between the upper margin of the radial head to the tip of the styloid process, palpable at the wrist thumb joint, using rod compass.
4. *Ulnar length (UL):* The left fore arm is flexed and semipronated with the hand in natural position. It is measured as a distance from the tip of the olecranon process to the distal margin of the ulnar head on the little

finger side, palpable on the dorsum of the wrist, using rod compass.

5. *Hand length (HL):* Subject's left hand is extended and placed on a horizontal platform with palm facing upwards. With the bar of the sliding caliper lying along the palm, the distance from the proximal bracelet crease to the tip of the left middle finger is measured, using sliding caliper.

Data on male and female Tangkhul Nagas have been subjected to statistical treatment to observe the sex differences between these body dimensions at the first instance and subsequently to compute Multiplication Factors (MFs) for estimation of stature from these dimensions of the upper extremity measures. In order to observe the validity of the MFs. formulated on Tangkhul Nagas 10 % data on males and females have been used to check the percentage error in the actual and the estimated stature for both male and female Tangkhul Nagas.

Results and Discussion

Analysis of data reveals that the male Tangkhul Nagas are not only taller than the females but they also have larger dimensions of the upper extremity measures than the females (Table-1). The sex differences as observed through t-test reveal highly significant variation between the sexes (p< 0.001).

Table 1
Mean and other statistical constants of upper extremity dimensions among male and female Tangkhul Nagas of Manipur

S. No.	*BODY DIMENSIONS*	*MALE*		*FEMALE*		*Value*
		Mean (cm)	*S.D.*	*Mean (cm)*		*of "t"*
1	Stature (S)	165.24	5.28	153.92	5.16	15.40 *
2	Upper arm length (UAL)	31.70	1.41	29.52	1.34	11.41*
3	Radial length (RL)	24.55	1.09	22.98	1.13	10.13*
4	Ulnar length (UL)	26.99	1.16	25.01	1.16	12.15*
5	Hand length (HL)	18.03	0.73	16.83	0.69	12.12*

* Significant at 0.01% level (P<0.001)

Table 2
Multiplication Factors for prediction of stature among Tangkhul Nagas of Manipur

S.No.	Body Dimensions	Multiplication Factors Male	Multiplication Factors Female
1	Upper arm length (UAL)	5.22	5.22
2	Radial length (RL)	6.74	6.71
3	Ulnar length (UL)	6.13	6.16
4	Hand length (HL)	9.30	9.15

Table-2 exhibits multiplication factors for all the body dimensions among male and female Tangkhul Nagas. It is observed that due to variation in the body proportions of male and female Tangkhul Nagas the value of multiplication factors is also variable for males and females except for upper arm length (UAL), which shows the same value of M.F. for both the sexes i.e., 5.22. The males show greater MFs. for radial length (RL) and hand length (HL) while females exhibit greater value of M.F. for ulnar length (UL). The difference between the MFs. for male and female Tangkhul Nagas varies from minimum 0.00 (in case of upper arm length) to a maximum of 0.15 (in case of hand length).

Table 3
Average Difference and Percentage Error in Actual and Estimated Stature using MFs. for all the measures of upper extremity among Tangkhul Nagas of Manipur

S. No.	Body Dimensions	Sex	M.Fs.	Average Difference	Percentage Error
1.	Upper arm length (UAL)	M	5.22	3.57	2.16
		F	5.22	4.07	2.64
2.	Radial length (RL)	M	6.74	3.28	1.98
		F	6.71	4.71	3.06
3.	Ulnar length (UL)	M	6.13	4.52	2.73
		F	6.16	3.90	2.53
4.	Hand length (HL)	M	9.30	3.82	2.31
		F	9.15	4.14	2.69

Table-3 presents the average difference and percentage error in actual and estimated stature using MFs. for all the four measures of upper extremity among Tangkhul Nagas.

It is observed that the average difference between actual and estimated stature is highest in case of ulnar length (UL) i.e., 4.52 among males while it is radial length (RL), which shows maximum average difference i.e., 4.71 in case of females.

The minimum average difference is observed in case of radial length (RL) among males i.e., 3.28 while ulnar length (UL) shows the lowest average difference among females i.e., 3.90

The percentage error works out to be below 3% for all the four measures in case of male while in case of female the percentage error works out to be 3% for all the upper extremity measures except radial length (RL) i.e., 3.06.

Among males the maximum percentage error is observed in case of ulnar length (i.e., 2.73) which is followed by HL (2.31), UAL (2.16) and RL (1.98) while among females RL exhibits the maximum percentage error (i.e.,3.06) which is followed by HL (2.69), UAL (2.64) and UL (2.53) .

Out of the four upper extremity measures the RL would provide the greater reliability in prediction of stature among males on using M.F. (which shows the lowest percentage error i.e., 1.98) while in case of females UL would provide the greater reliability in estimation of stature (which shows the least percentage error i.e., 2.53).

Thus, stature of recently death or decomposed or partly mutilated death body who happens to be male or female Tangkhul Nagas of Manipur could be predicted on using the MFs. formulated for all the four upper extremity dimensions (i.e., UAL, RL, UL and HL) for either sex.

REFERENCES

ALLBROOK, D. 1961. The estimation of stature in British and East African males based on tibial and ulnar bone length. *J. For. Med., 8:* 15 – 28.

ANAND, S. and S. Nath. 1990. Estimation of stature through percutaneous measures of upper and lower extremities among Rajputs of Pauri Garhwal. *Ind. J. For. Sci., 5:* 83- 89.

DEVI, L.S. 2001. Estimation of stature from different body dimensions among Meiteis of Manipur. Unpublished Ph.D. Thesis, Univ. Delhi.

DEVI, L.S. and S. NATH, 2001. Prediction of stature among male Meiteis of Manipur Through hand, foot and facial dimensions. Proceeding Volume of National Conference on advances in *Forensic Science, Delhi. (8th -10th Jan., 2001):* 117-121. 5.

DUGGAL, N. and S. NATH. 1986. Estimation of stature using percutaneous lengths of radius, ulna and tibia among Lodhas and Mundas of District Midnapore, West Bengal. *Anthropologie, 24:* 23-27.

GARG, R. 1987. Reconstruction of stature using certain body measurements among Rajput males and females of District Dehradun, Uttar Pradesh. Unpublished Master's Dissertation, Uni. Delhi.

JOHNSTONE, J.1896. *My experience in Manipur and Naga Hills.*

KAUR, S. 1996. Reconstruction of stature through measurements of upper and lower extremities among male and female Rajputs of Sirmour District, Himachal Pradesh. Unpublished Master's Dissertation, Univ. of Delhi.

KAUR, S. and S. NATH. 1997. Reconstruction of stature from various dimensions of upper extremity among Sikh females of Delhi. *Proceedings of Xth All India Forensic Science Conference, Bhubaneswar, (11th—3th Nov., 1997):* 6-60.

KLER, G.S., N.A. BUTT and P.K. CHATTOPADHYAY. 1992. Estimation of stature from nasal height. *Ind. J. For. Sci., 6:* 87-93.

MARTIN, R and SALLER. 1959. Lehrbuch der Anthropologie in Systematischer. Fischer Darstellung, Stuttgart.

NATH, S. 1993. Anthropometry—The Measurement of Body Size, Shape and Form. Friends Publication, Delhi.

NATH, S. 1997. Estimation of stature through hand and foot lengths among Jats of Rajasthan. *Police Research and Development Journal. Qr. IV:* 20-22.

NATH, S. and G. KRISHAN. 1990. Determination of stature using percutaneous measurements of upper and lower limbs among Hindu (Baniya) females of Delhi. *J. Anthrop. Soc. India, 39:* 151-166.

NATH, S. and N.S. CHANDRA.1986. Computation of new MFs. for stature estimation from percutaneous lengths of radius and tibia. *Police Research and Development Journal, Qr. I:* 13-15.

NATH, S. and S. KAUR.1998. Reconstruction of stature through percutaneous measurements of upper and lower limb bone length among Rajputs of District Sirmour, H.P. *South Asian Anthropologist, 19:* 57-63.

Nath, S., RAJANI and S. CHHIBBER. 1990. Reconstruction of stature from percutaneous length of upper and lower extremity segments among Punjabi females of Delhi. *Ind. J. For. Sci., 4:* 171-181.

SETHI, V. 1998. Determination of stature on the basis of percutaneous measures of upper and lower extremities among Punjabi and Jain females of Delhi. Unpublished M. Phil. Dissertation, Univ. Delhi.

19

Reconstruction of Stature Among Jains of Delhi through Lower Limb Dimensions

*Surinder Nath**
*Preeti Jain***
*Bhavna****

Abstract

The present study pertains to formulation of multiplication factors (M.F.) for estimation of stature among male and female Jains of Delhi using four dimensions of lower limb pertaining to lengths of femur, tibia, fibula and foot.

Data for the present study consists of a total 1006 adult Jains (468 males and 538 females) ranging in age range 17-40 years for females and 18-40 years for males of Delhi. All the subjects were measured for the four lower limb dimensions besides stature in accordance with the standard techniques.

Analyses reveal that tibial length among males and femoral length among females provide the best estimate of

* Department of Anthropology, University of Delhi, Delhi 110 007

stature among the Jains of Delhi as observed through the percentage error.

Introduction

The identification of skeletal remains badly decomposed or mutilated unidentified human remains, is important for both legal and humanitarian reasons. Forensic anthropologists apply standard scientific techniques developed in physical anthropology to identify such remains, and to assist in the detection of crime.

Reconstruction of stature occupies a relatively central position in the process Of identification initiated by forensic and medico legal experts. Out of the two methods advocated by Thomas Dwight *(1894), i.e.* Anatomical and Mathematical, for estimation of stature from Skeletonized remains, mathematical method has universal applicability over the anatomical method because it is workable even with a single bone as against anatomical one where the whole skeleton is required for estimation of stature.

Due to non availability of documented skeletal material in India Allbrook's (1961) alternative method of using the percutaneous measurements of limb bones to formulate means of stature reconstruction is followed (Athwale, 1963; Patel et al., 1964; Joshi et al., 1964, 1965; Kolte and Bansal, 1974; Duggal and Nath, 1986; Nath et al., 1988, 1990; Anand and Nath, 1990; Nath and Krishan, 1990; Nath and Rautray, 1996; Jain et al., 1996; Jain and Nath, 1997; Nath and Kaur, 1998, Jain et al., 1999; Sethi and Nath, 2001; Devi and Nath, 2001).

In the present study a similar attempt has been made to compute multiplication factors for reconstruction of stature among a living population, the Jains, of Delhi, using percutaneous lengths of the femur, tibia and fibula besides using foot length for this purpose.

Material and Methods

A total 1006 adult Jains (468 males and 538 females) ranging in age 17-40 years for females and 18-40 years for males, of

Delhi have been measured for the following measurements as per the techniques recommended by Martin and Saller (1959), Allbrook (1961), and Weiner and Lourie (1969):

1. *Stature (S):* It is obtained as the projective distance between the standing surface and the highest point on the head (vertex) when the subject is standing in the standard standing position, using anthropometric rod.
2. *Femur Length (FEML):* Subject stands erect with the left leg placed slightly ahead of the right one and the foot partly inverted to relax the soft tissues. Using the rod compass, measure the distance from the upper most point on the greater trochanter to the lower most point palpable on the lateral femoral condyle.
3. *Tibial Length (TIBL):* Subject sat with left knee placed in the semi-flexed position and the left foot partly inverted to relax the soft tissues and render bony landmarks prominent. Using the rod compass, length of tibia from the medial condyle (as it becomes palpable and diverges anteriorly from the articulating femoral condyle) to the tip of the medial malleolus, is measured.
4. *Fibular Length (FIBL):* Subject sat with left knee placed in the semi-flexed position and the left foot partly inverted to relax the soft tissues and render bony landmarks prominent. Using the rod compass, the distance between the upper most point palpable on fibular head, little below the lateral margin of the knee and the tip of the lateral malleolus, is measured.
5. *Foot Length (FL):* Subject stands erect with left foot placed twelve inches ahead of the right one with entire weight of body falling on left foot. Using the rod compass, measure the distance between Acropodion and Pternion when the foot is fully stretched.

Data have been subjected to statistical analysis to observe the sex differences in these body dimensions and for computation of multiplication factors for reconstruction of stature from femur, tibial, fibular and foot lengths, separately for male and female Jains.

Results and Discussion

Preliminary analysis of the data reveals that the male Jains are not only taller than the females but they also have relatively longer limb bone dimensions and foot length (Table 1). The differential trends as assessed through t-test reveal highly significant sex differences ($p<0.001$) for all the bone and body dimensions.

Keeping in view the highly significant sex differences the data on male and female Jains have been processed independently for computation of Multiplication Factors (MFs) for prediction of stature from these bone and body dimensions (Table 2). It is apparent from the table that owing to the variation observed in the bone and body dimensions among the sexes the MFs for FEML and FIBL are slightly greater for males while for TIBL and FL they are greater for females. This variation clearly indicates that it would not be appropriate to use these MFs interchangeably.

With a view to observe the reliability of these MFs formulated for Jains of Delhi a fresh data were collected on 100 Jains amounting to nearly 10 percent of the total sample size (50 males and 50 females) ranging in age from 20 to 40 years. Using all the MFs stature was calculated for both male and female Jains to observe the difference between the actual and estimated stature and to assess the percentage error in the estimated stature. Table 3 reveals the average difference between the actual and the estimated stature on using MFs for FEML, TIBL, FIBL and FL. It is observed that the average difference works out to be between 4.3 cm and 5.2 cm in case of males whole among females it ranges from 4.4 cm to 5.0 cm. The percentage error calculated on the basis of average difference and the actual stature comes out to be less than 3 percent in all the cases except for females with TIBL and for males with FL where it exceeds beyond 3 percent. However the least percentage error is observed as 2.58 percent for males on using MF for TIBL and 2.77 percent for females on using MF for FEML. It may be pointed out here that for individual dimensions the percentage error is greater for males on using FEML and FL in comparison to females. On the other hand TIBL and

FIBL exhibit greater percentage error for females. As the percentage error is less than 3 percent in most cases these MFs could be used to predict stature with reasonable accuracy for Jains of Delhi.

It has been reported by certain researchers (Stevenson, 1929; Nath, 1996; Kodagoda and Jayasinghe, 1998) that the means of stature reconstruction are not only sex specific but are also population specific and thus the multiplication factors or the regression equations formulated for one population groups must not be used to predict stature of another as it would yield improper estimate of stature. To further prove this aspect an attempt has been made in the present study to enlist Multiplication Factors available on various Indian population groups for FEML. TIBL, FEML and FL for either sex.

Table 4 presents a comparative account of MFs reported on a total of 39 Indian living Population groups (18 male and 21 female). It is observed that out of 39 populations listed MF for FEML is available for only 28 (12 male and 16 female). The MF for males varies from 3.16 among Rajputs of Garhwal to 4.42 among Rajputs of Ranikhet. The Jain males of the present study with MF as 4.06 fall well within this range. The MF for females, on the other hand, ranges between 3.33 among Brahmins of Garhwal and 4.05 among Meiteis of Manipur. The female Jains of the present study with the MF as 3.99 are relatively close to the upper limit of the range for the females.

MFs for TIBL are available on all the 39 populations listed in the table. It may be noted that for males the MF value ranges between 4.00 among Yadavs of Delhi and 5.21 among Rajputs of Ranikhet, while for females it varies between 4.15 among Mundas of West Bengal and 4.76 among Rajputs of Garhwal. The male and the female Jains of the present study with their MFS as 4.47 and 4.49 respectively are well within the minimum and maximum range of the MF for TIBL.

In comparison to FEML and TIBL, Fibular length appears to be a less common or important bone dimension for reconstruction of stature as out of 39 populations, MFs for

FIBL are reported on only 14 populations (7 male and 7 female). The MF for males fluctuate between 4.11 among Jats of Churu and 4.81 among Rajputs of Ranikhet. In case of females it ranges from 4.13 among Jats of Churu to 4.44 among Rajputs of Sirmour. Male Jains of the present study with the MF as 4.44 are well within the range while the females of the present study with the MF as 4.43 are almost close to the maximum limit of the range.

Table 4 further lists the MF values of FL for estimation of stature for 31 population groups (13 male and 18 female). It is apparent that among males the MF value varies from a minimum of 6.18 among Brahmins of Garhwal to a maximum of 7.83 among Brahmins of Ranikhet. The male Jains of the present study with the MF as 6.62 fall well within the range.

MF for females, on the other hand fluctuate between 6.26 among Mundas of West Bengal and 7.28 among Rajputs of Dehradun.The female Jains of the present study with their MF as 6.75 fall well within the minimum and maximum range.

It is quite clear from this comparative table that the MF values for FEML, TIBL, FIBL and FL not only differ between the sexes but also between population groups to a large extent.

However there are a few cases where the MF values of different population groups /sexes may be identical for a specific bone or body dimension. Despite such a similarity it is essential to formulate MFs for each population and sex to avoid enhancing the extent of error in the estimated stature as has already been demonstrated by different researchers (Stevenson, 1929; Kodagoda and Jayasinghe, 1998 and Jain, 1999).

However, to achieve still greater precision in the estimated stature one could develop regression formulae for each of these dimensions as they reduce the percentage of error to a significant extent. But this does reduce the utility of the MFs for the simple reason they are handier in comparison to the regression equations and can be used right at the crime scene to have an estimate of stature almost instantaneously.

REFERENCES

ALLBROOK, D. 1961. The estimation of stature in British and East African males based on tibial and ulnar bone lengths. *J. For. Med., 8:* 15-28.

ANAND, N. and S. NATH. 1990. Estimation of stature through percutaneous measures of the upper and lower extremities among Rajputs of Pauri Garhwal. *Ind. J. For. Sci., 5:* 83-89.

ATHAWALE, M.C. 1963. Estimation of height from lengths of forearm bones: A Study of One Hundred Maharashtrians Male Adults of Ages between Twenty-five and Thirty years. *Am. J. Phys. Anthrop., 21:* 105-112.

DEVI, L. SUNITA and S. NATH. 2001. Prediction of stature among male Meiteis of Manipur through hand, foot and facial dimensions. In Advances in *Forensic Science.*

Eds M.K. Bhasin and Surinder Nath. Department of Anthropology, University of Delhi, Delhi-110007.

DUGGAL, N. and S. NATH. 1986. Estimation of stature using percutaneous length of radius, ulna and tibia among Lodhas and Mundas of District Midnapore, West Bengal. *Anthropologie, 24:* 23-27.

DWIGHT, T. 1894. Methods of estimating the height from parts of the skeleton. *Med. Rec. N.Y., 46:* 293-296.

JAIN, P. 1999. Estimation of Stature from various body dimensions among Jains of Delhi. Unpublished Thesis. University of Delhi, Delhi-110007.

JAIN, P., S. KAUR and S. NATH.1996. Reconstruction of stature from hand and foot dimensions among male Brahmins of Kumaon. *J. Ind. Acad. For. Sci., 35:* 22-29.

JAIN, P. and S. NATH. 1997. Estimation of stature through upper and lower limb dimensions among Brahmins of Kumaon. *Ind. J. Phys. Anthrop. and Hum. Gent. 20:* 163-168.

JAIN, P., S. ROY and S. NATH.1999. Estimation of stature through measurements of hand and foot among female Jats of Delhi. *Anthropologist, 1:* 171-173..

JOSHI, N.B., M.P. PATEL and A.V. DONGRE. 1964. Regression equation of height on ulnar length. *Ind. J. Med. Res., 52:* 1088-1091.

JOSHI, N.B., M.P. PATEL, M.G. AMIN and A.V. DONGRE.1965. Use of tibia and ulna in estimation of total body height. *Ind. J. Med. Res. 53:* 831-834.

KODAGODA, N. and S. JAYASINGHE. 1998. A preliminary test of Pearson's formula for estimation of height of Sri Lankans. *For. Sci. Int., 36:* 241-246.

KOLTE, P.M. and P.C. BANSAL.1974. Determination of regression formulae for reconstruction of stature from the long bones of upper limb in Maharashtrians of Marathwada region. *J. Anat. Soc. Ind., 23:* 1-11.

MARTIN, R. and K.. SALLER. 1959. Lehrbuch der Anthropologie in Systematischer. Fischer Darstellung, Stuttgart.

NATH, S. 1996. Forensic Anthropology. Ashtam Prakashan. Delhi.

NATH, S., N. DUGGAL and *N.S. CHANDRA*.1988. Reconstruction of stature on the basis of percutaneous length of forearm bones among the Munda of Midnapore District, West Bengal. *Hum. Sci., 37:* 170-175.

NATH, S. and S. KAUR.1998. Reconstruction of stature through percutaneous measurements of upper and lower limb bone lengths among Rajputs of District Sirmour, H. P. *South Asian Anthropologist, 19: 57-63.*

NATH, S. and G. KRISHAN.1990. Determination of stature using percutaneous measurements of upper and lower limb bones among Hindu (Baniya) females of *Delhi J. Anthrop. Survey of Ind.,* 39: 151-156.

NATH, S., RAJNI and S. CHHIBBER.1990. Reconstruction of stature from percutaneous lengths of upper and lower extremity segments among Punjabi females of Delhi. *Ind. J. For. Sci., 4:* 171-181.

PATEL, M.P., N. B. JOSHI and A.V. DONGRE. 1964. Regression equation of height on tibial length. *Ind. J. Med. Res., 52:* 531-534.

SETHI, V. and S. NATH. 2001. Prediction of stature using upper limb bone dimensions among Jain females of Delhi. In *Advances in Forensic Science.* Eds. M.K.Bhasin and *Surinder Nath,* Department of Anthropology, University of Delhi, Delhi-110007.

STEVENSON, P.H. 1929. On racial differences in stature long bone regression formulae with special reference to stature reconstruction formulae for the Chinese. *Biom., 21:* 303-318.

WEINER, J.S. and J.A. LOURIE.1969. Human Biology: A Guide to Field Methods. IBP Handbook No.9, Blackwell Scientific Publications, Oxford.

Table 1

Sex differences in different dimensions of lower extremity and stature among Jains of Delhi

S.No.	Measurement	Males Mean (cm)	SEx	Females Mean (cm)	SEx	Value of t
1.	Stature (S)	166.57	0.27	158.28	0.22	23.91*
2.	Femur Length (FEML)	41.19	0.10	39.48	0.09	12.85*
3.	Tibial Length (TIBL)	37.28	0.09	34.39	0.08	24.32*
4.	Fibular Length (FIBL)	37.55	0.09	34.86	0.08	22.35*
5.	Foot Length	25.21	0.06	22.88	0.05	28.07*

* Highly significant at 0.01% level (p<0.001)

Table 2

Multiplication Factors of Lower extremity dimensions among Jains

S.No.	Measurement	Multiplication Factors Males	Females
1.	FEML	4.06	3.92
2.	TIBL	4.47	4.49
3.	FIBL	4.44	4.43
4.	FL	6.62	6.75

Table 3

Assessment of percentage error in actual and estimated stature on using MFs on a fresh sample of 50 male and 50 female Jains

S.No.	Measurement	Sex	Average Difference (cm)	Percentage Error
1	FEML	Male	4.7	2.82
		Female	4.4	2.77
2	TIBL	Male	4.3	2.58
		Female	5.0	3.15
3.	FIBL	Male	4.4	2.64
		Female	4.7	2.97
4.	FL	Male	5.2	3.12
		Female	4.6	2.90

Table 4
Multiplication Factors for different lower extremity dimensions among various living population groups of India

S.No.	Population/ Sex/ Region	Author/Year	Multiplication Factor			
			FEML	TIBL	FIBL	FL
1.	Munda (M) W.Bengal	Duggal&Nath 1986	-	4.16	-	6.24
2.	Munda (F) W.Bengal	Duggal&Nath, 1986	-	4.15	-	6.26
3.	Lodha (M) W.Bengal	Duggal&Nath, 1986	-	4.21	-	6.45
4.	Lodha (F) W.Bengal	Duggal&Nath, 1986	-	4.23	-	6.32
5.	Bhil (M) Udaipur	Nath&Chandra, 1986	-	4.27	-	-
6.	Brahmin (M) Ranikhet	Tiwary, 1986	4.14	5.20	4.80	7.83
7.	Rajput (M) Ranikhet	Tiwary, 1986	4.42	5.21	4.81	7.46
8.	Rajput (M) Dehradun	Garg, 1987	-	4.43	-	6.66
9	Rajput (F) Dehradun	Garg, 1987	-	4.34	-	7.28
10.	Brahmin (M) Garhwal	Anand, 1990	3.32	4.59	-	6.18
11.	Brahmin (F) Garhwal	Anand, 1990	3.33	4.43	-	6.79
12.	Rajput (M) Garhwal	Anand & Nath, 1990	3.16	4.52	-	6.42
13.	Rajput (F) Garhwal	Anand & Nath, 1990	3.37	4.76	-	7.13
14	Hindu Baniya (F) Delhi	Nath&Krishan, 1990	3.53	4.39	-	6.64
15.	Punjabi (F) Delhi	Nath et al., 1990	3.54	4.46	-	6.67
16.	Jat (M) Churu	Rautray, 1995	3.91	4.10	4.11	6.60
17.	Jat (F) Churu	Rautray, 1995	3.97	4.20	4.13	6.68
18.	Brahmin (M) Kumaon	Jain & Nath, 1997	3.75	4.30	-	-
19.	Sikh (M) Delhi	Kaur, 1998	3.84	4.32	4.16	6.60
20.	Sikh (F) Delhi	Kaur, 1998	3.77	4.34	4.15	6.79
21.	Rajput (M) Sirmour	Nath & Kaur, 1998	4.01	4.33	4.45	-
22.	Rajput (F) Sirmour	Nath & Kaur, 1998	3.98	4.35	4.44	-
23.	Bengali Sudra (F) Delhi	Nath et al., 1998	3.47	4.49	-	6.67
24.	Bengali Brahmin (F) Delhi	Nath et al., 1998	3.50	4.46	-	6.68
25.	Brahmin (M) Pithoragarh	Sachdeva et al, 1998	-	4.28	-	-
26.	Brahmin (F) Pithoragarh	Sachdeva et al, 1998	-	4.30	-	-
27.	Rajput (M) Pithoragarh	Sachdeva et al, 1998	-	4.42	-	-
28.	Rajput (F) Pithoragarh	Sachdeva et al, 1998	-	4.37	-	-
29.	Punjabi (F) Delhi	Sethi, 1998	3.76	4.53	4.35	6.79
30.	Jain (F) Delhi	Sethi, 1998	3.70	4.55	4.34	6.83
31.	Warli (M) Maharashtra	Jain et al, 1999	3.55	4.23	-	6.49
32.	Warli (F) Maharashtra	Jain et al. 1999	5.27	4.31	-	6.58
33.	Bengali Badiyas (F) Delhi	Nath et al, 1999	3.36	4.40	-	6.79
34.	Bengali Kayasthas (F) Delhi	Nath et al, 1999	3.45	4.42	-	6.68
35.	Yadav (M) Delhi	Nath et al, 1999	3.34	4.00	-	6.63
36.	Meiteis (M) Manipur	Devi, 2001	4.04	4.62	4.42	6.80
37.	Meiteis (F) Manipur	Devi, 2001	4.05	4.59	4.40	6.88
38.	Jain (M) Delhi	Present Study	4.06	4.47	4.44	6.62

20

Executant Genuine But Agreement Forged

*Vikram Raj Singh Chauhan**

Abstract

It is a very typical case of forgery in which the executant admit her signature but not the typewritten agreement. The Plaintiff Ashwani Kumar had procured the signature of Balwant Kaur on blank stamp paper of Rs. 10 which she might have signed for some other purpose or in good faith and made an false typewritten agreement of sale of her house and same was denied by the defendant Balwant Kaur except her signatures on it. The Plaintiff is having the strong case who has only to prove the genuineness of the signatures of defendant, which she had already admitted, with his own witnesses. The defendant consulted the author who thoroughly examined the spacing between body type writings, alignment of words, lines, paragraphs, dot above and tick mark below signature of Balwant Kaur, characteristic arrow mark, some letters typed and then scored off, examination of ink of signatures and above all

* Chief Forensic Investigator, Patiala Bureau of Identification, Patiala and President North Zone Forensic Science Association, India.

the conscious of the typist/forger and came to conclusion that the forger/typist had left enough evidence to prove himself that the agreement is a clear cut piece of forgery despite the genuine signature of defendant.

Introduction

A suit for specific performance of the agreement to sell dated 27.7.98 was filed in the Court by the Plaintiff Ashwani Kumar against the defendant Balwant Kaur alleging that the defendant had agreed to sell her house for consideration of Rs. 3,00,000 and had received a sum of Rs. 1,00,000 from the plaintiff in cash as earnest money and executed an agreement to sell but the defendant Balwant Kaur failed to execute and register the sale deed in favor of the plaintiff as per the agreement. On the other hand defendant alleged that she had not executed any agreement in favor of plaintiff and in fact she had taken the loan of Rs. 50,000 from Sanjiv Kumar, the brother of the plaintiff and had repaid the loan amount with interest. The defendant also stated that Sanjiv Kumar at the time of giving the loan got some blank stamp papers signed from her and also kept the original sale deed of her house as a security which he refused to return even after the payment of loan amount. The defendant had also registered a complaint against Sanjiv Kumar and it might be possible that Sanjiv Kumar had handed over the blank stamp papers to his real brother Ashwani Kumar, the plaintiff, who had converted one of the blank stamp paper into agreement of sale in his favor and thus the alleged agreement to sell is forged and fabricated document. The plaintiff had produced two witnesses of the agreement to prove his case and one document expert who stated that the agreement is a genuine document. On the other hand the defendant consulted the author to examine the disputed agreement in order to ascertain whether the signature of Balwant Kaur, the executant, was already there on the blank stamp paper and the agreement was typed in gurmukhi later on or not?

Material and Methods

The Agreement was examined and compared with the help of photographs taken with close up lenses, epidiascope, universal dactyloscopic outfits, falmer magnifiers, microscopic lenses, microscopes and other necessary instruments.

Discussions and Results

In the first instance, I compared the body type writings of the disputed agreement interse and I have noted that the first paragraph after the word "Ikrarnama" (Agreement) is started from the extreme left side and the Ist & IInd lines are typed incompletely despite enough space is available on the right side. The second paragraph is started after leaving a space on the left side. Thus the alignment of paragraphs is not similar in this disputed agreement showing that the typist as conscious from the very beginning.

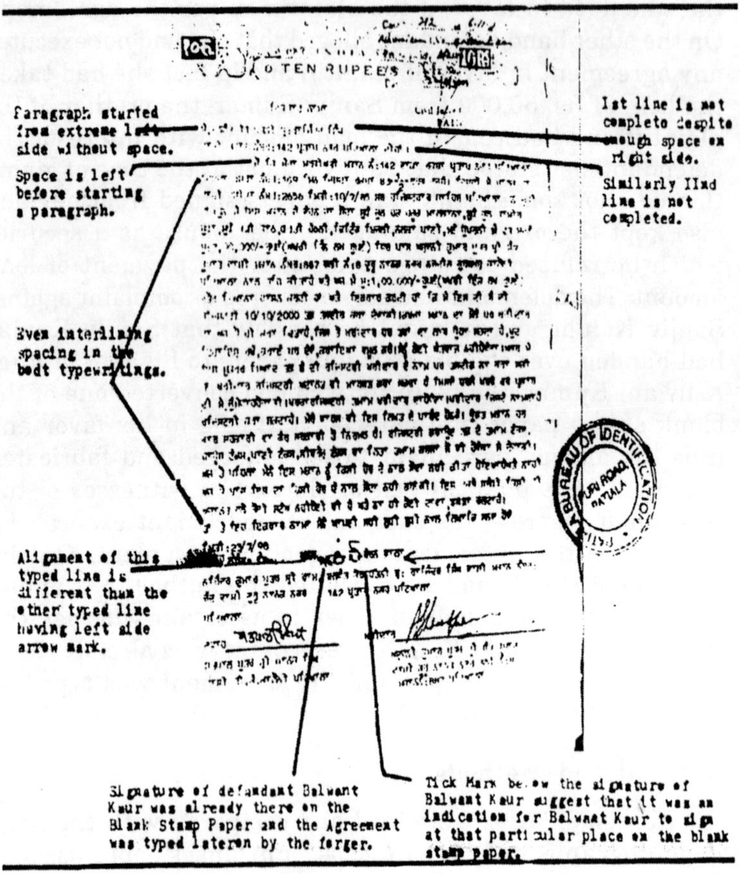

Secondly the interlining spacing between the typed lines is even in the body type writings up to the word "Hovey" but after this there is an comparatively more space between the last typed line and the date portion. Thereafter there is very less space between the date portion and the word "Gawah".

Thirdly the line typed for signing the witness Narinder Kumar is very short as compared to the other typed lines for the reasons that the signature of Balwant Kaur was already there on the blank stamp paper otherwise the typed line must had been longer as that was typed for witness Satpal.

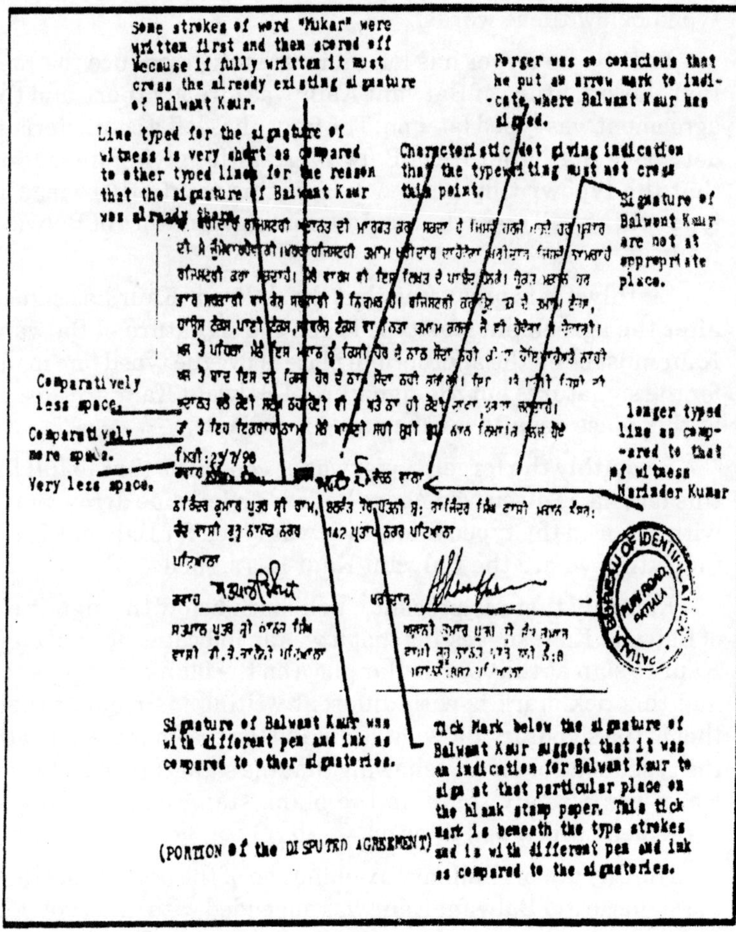

(PORTION of the DISPUTED AGREEMENT)

Fourthly after typing the short type line for the witness Narinder Kumar the typist had typed the word "Mukar" which means executant and thereafter this word is scored off by typing "XXX" as there was a difficulty for the typist to make a typed line below the already existing signature of Balwant Kaur. But an idea came to the mind of the forger/typist and he typed the word "Veychan Wala" inspite of the word "Mukar" after the already existing signature of Balwant Kaur and here he made the typed line below that word for making the proper sequence and in this effort he made the uneven alignment between the word "Gawah" and word "Veychan wala" and in the typed lines typed below these words.

Fifthly the forger has left an interesting evidence to prove that the signature of Balwant Kaur was already there and the agreement was typed later on. The forger has left a characteristic dot above the signature of Balwant Kaur for giving indication that the typewriting must not cross this point otherwise the typewriting will cross the already existing signature of Balwant Kaur.

Sixthly if it is presumed that the Balwant Kaur has signed after the agreement was typed then the signature of Balwant Kaur must be on the appropriate place above the typed line made for the signatures but the signature of Balwant Kaur are absent at this place despite much space is available.

Seventhly the forger/typist was so conscious that to full fill this lacuna as discussed above he made a left side arrow mark with a pen on the typed line which was typed for Balwant Kaur indicating where the Balwant Kaur has signed.

Eighthly there is present a tick mark below the signature of Balwant Kaur suggesting that it was an indication for Balwant Kaur to sign at that particular place on the blank stamp paper and this tick mark is with different writing instrument than that of the signatory Balwant Kaur and the tick mark is beneath the typed matter clearly showing that the signature of Balwant Kaur was already there on the blank stamp paper and the agreement was typed later on.

Ninthly the preliminary examination of the ink reveals that the signature of Balwant Kaur was appended with different pen and ink as compared to that of other signatories. The signature of Balwant Kaur is with dark blackish blue ink while the signatures of other signatories are with light blue ink clearly showing the difference with an naked eye.

Conclusion

After considering the above points with proper reasoning, I am of the opinion that the signature of Balwant Kaur was already there on the blank stamp paper and the agreement dated 23.7.98 was typed later on by the typist/forger and as such the disputed agreement dated 23.7.98, is a forged document.

REFERENCES

1. Ashwani Kumar versus Balwant Kaur: Suit for Specific performance & Permanent Injunction of year 2000, Court of Civil Judge (Senior Division), Patiala.
2. Brewester, F: *Contested Documents & Forgeries,* Book Company Ltd., Calcutta, 1932.
3. Hilton, O.: *Scientific Examination of Questioned Documents,* Elsevier North Holland Inc., New York, 1982.
4. Harrison, W. R: *Suspected Documents—Their Scientific Examination,* Sweet and Maxwell Limited, London, 1966. Reprinted in 1996.
5. Lloyd L. Jones: *Valid or forged,* Funk & Wagnalis, New York & London Company, 1938.
6. Mehta, M.K.: *Expert Testimony in Typewriting,* Delhi, 1954.
7. Newton, Baker J.: *Law of Disputed & Forged Documents,* The Michie Company Charlottesville, Virginia, 1955.
8. Osborn, A.S.: *Questioned Documents,* Nelson Hall Co., Chicago, 1929.
9. Puri, Jagjit: Forger is smart but the Expert Smarter Selected works of Dewan K.S. Puri on Disputed Handwriting and Finger Prints Comparison, Dewan K.S. Puri Foundation, Patiala, 2003.
10. Rhodes, Henry T.F.: *The Craft of Forgery,* London, 1934.
11. Saxsena, B.L.: Law and Techniques relating to Identification of Handwriting, Disputed Documents, Finger Prints, Foot Prints and Detection of Forgeries, Central Law Agency, Allahabad, 1990.
12. Srivastva, Ram Prasad & Hardless Charles E.: *Case Law on Expert Evidence,* Allahabad, 1934.

21

Can the Departed Soul Be Lived Again

*Vikram Raj Singh Chauhan**

Abstract

This is a very interesting case of child rebirth. In this case a six year old boy Taranjit Singh of Alluna Miana Village, Distt. Ludhiana claimed that he remembers his previous life. He said that he was born in Chakkchela village in Jalandhar District and his name was Satnam Singh and was a student of IX class in a school in Nihalwal Village. The author became curious to know the incident of rebirth and went to villages Alluna miana and Chakkchela to confirm the incident scientifically. The author took the specimen writings of Taranjit Singh (after incarnation) both in Gurmukhi and Roman Script and also the writings of Satnam Singh from the copy books kept by the family of Satnam Singh, to know whether the handwritings of Satnam Singh and Taranjit Singh are Corresponding or not? It may be noted that the handwriting

* Chief Forensic Investigator, Patiala Bureau of Identification, Patiala and President North Zone Forensic Science Association, India.

is not only a design of letters but also has specific mannerism of writing based on the inner writing characteristics, which help to distinguish one handwriting from another. Acting upon the above principle it was utter surprise to author that the handwritings of Taranjit Singh were corresponding with that of Satnam Singh except the difference in the muscular coordination of the writer Taranjit Singh as he was not accustomed to write but otherwise individual characteristics were corresponding. Thus on the basis of handwriting comparison it can be said scientifically that the departed soul of Satnam Singh has been transferred into Taranjit Singh and lived again.

Introduction

This is a very interesting case of child rebirth. In this case a six year old by Taranjit Singh of Alluna Miana Village, Distt. Ludhiana claimed that he remembers his previous life. He said that he was born in Chakkchela village in Jalandhar District and his name was Satnam Singh and his father's name was Jeet Singh. He was a student of class IX in a school in Nihalwal Village at the time of his death when on that fateful day of 10.9.92, he as returning home on bicycle from his school along with his friend Sukhwinder Singh; when a scooter rider named Joga Singh of village Mirajwala, Tehsil Shahkot, hit him. He received serious injuries on his head and died the following day. His present father Ranjit Singh told that the boy started demanding to be taken to Chakkchela village when he was just one and a half year old. Ranjit Singh and his friend Rajinder Singh Went to Govt. school in Nihalwal village in Jalandhar Distt and enquired from an old teacher who told that it was true that a boy named Satnam Singh had died in an accident and that he was the son of Jeet Singh at Chakkchela village. Then the family reached the house of Jeet Singh and narrated the whole story. Ranjit Singh also told that his son says that the books (kept by her previous mother) bears blood stains and his purse contains Rs. 30. On listening this previous mother of Taranjit started weeping and confirmed his claim. After few days Taranjit Singh's previous life brother Kewal Singh, sister Lakhvir Kaur, friend

Buta Singh, previous father Jeet Singh and mother Mohinder Kaur came to Alluna Miana village to meet Taranjit. His previous sister Lakhvir Kaur had shown the photograph of her marriage to Taranjit Singh and asked him to recognize his previous birth photograph. Taranjit Singh immediately recognized the same and also the photo of his previous parents.

The Author became curious to know the incident of rebirth and went to villages Alluna Miana and Chakkchela along with his team of associate experts to confirm the truth. Both the families repeated the same above story.

Material and Methods

To confirm the incident scientifically the author took the specimen writings of Taranjit Singh (after incarnation) both in Gurmukhi and Roman Script and also the writings of Satnam Singh from the copy books kept by the family of Satnam Singh and authenticated by the school authorities, to know whether the handwriting of Satnam Singh and Taranjit Singh is corresponding or not? Both the sets of handwritings were examined and compared, in various sittings, with the help of photographs taken with close up lenses, epidiascope, universal dactyloscopic outfits, falmer magnifiers, microscopic lenses, microscopes and other necessary instruments.

Discussions and Results

It may be noted that the handwriting is not only a design of letters but also has specific mannerism of writing based on the inner writing characteristics, which help to distinguish one handwriting from another.

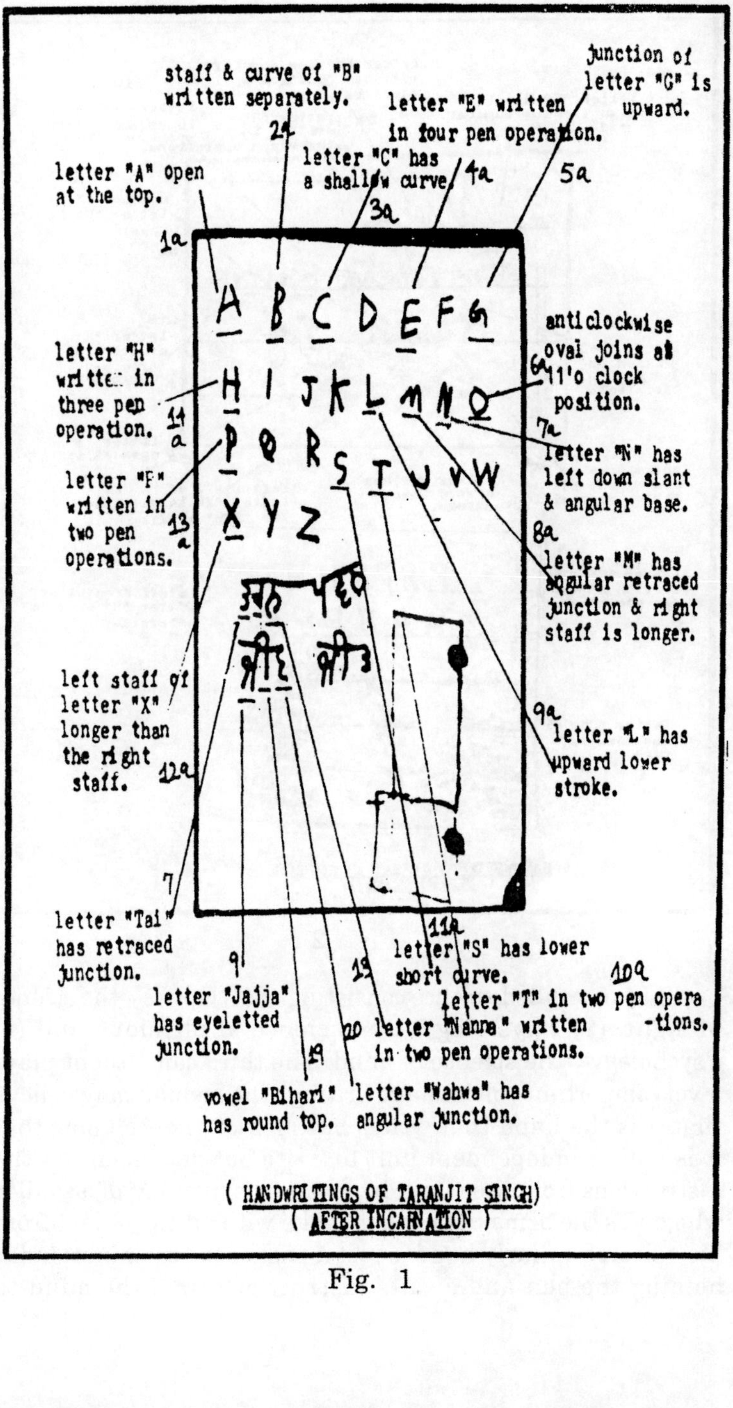
staff & curve of "B" written separately.
junction of letter "G" is upward.
letter "E" written in four pen operation.
letter "C" has a shallow curve.
letter "A" open at the top.
1a
2a
3a
4a
5a
A B C D E F G
H I J K L M N O
P Q R S T U V W
X Y Z
anticlockwise oval joins at 11'o clock position.
6a
letter "H" written in three pen operation.
14 a
letter "P" written in two pen operations.
13 a
7a
letter "N" has left down slant & angular base.
8a
letter "M" has angular retraced junction & right staff is longer.
left staff of letter "X" longer than the right staff.
12a
9a
letter "L" has upward lower stroke.
7
letter "Tai" has retraced junction.
9
11a
letter "S" has lower short curve.
10a
letter "T" in two pen opera -tions.
letter "Jajja" has eyeletted junction.
19
20
letter "Nanna" written in two pen operations.
vowel "Bihari" has round top.
letter "Wahwa" has angular junction.
(HANDWRITINGS OF TARANJIT SINGH)
(AFTER INCARNATION)

Fig. 1

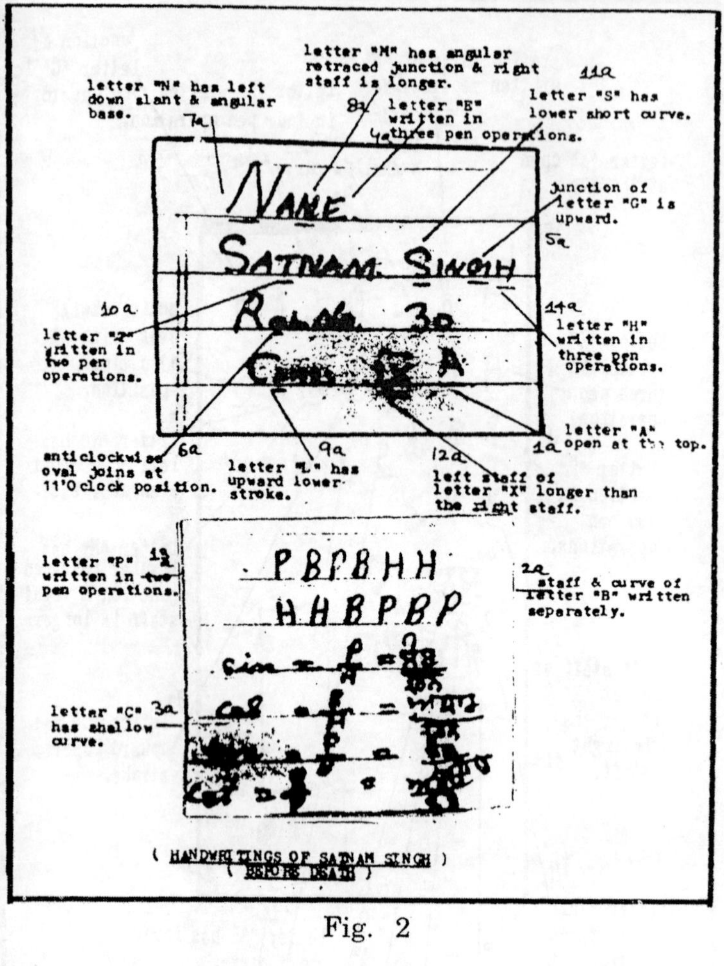

Fig. 2

It is an applied science consisting of (1) Optics—the science of sight, (2) Physiology—the science of physique and (3) Psychology—the science of mind. The third constituent plays a very important role in handwriting. The layman may believe that it is the hand that writes but men of science know that it is not an independent unit to write but dependent on the instructions from the mind. Its position is like that of a soldier who holds the arms but cannot strike without the orders from his officer. Similarly hand is just a part of the combination for holding the pen and awaits instructions from the mind to muscles to react for the desired task. Thus the mind plays an important role in handwriting and the hand only translates into action the dictates of the mind which cannot be the same in two different writers.

Now let us apply this principle in the two sets of handwriting i.e. one belongs to the deceased Satnam Singh and the other belongs to the alive Taranjit Singh who claims himself to be Satnam Singh who died in the year 1992.

Acting upon the above principle, it was utter surprise to me that the handwritings of Taranjit Singh corresponding with the of Satnam Singh except the difference in the muscular coordination of the writer Taranjit Singh as he was not costumed to write but otherwise individual characteristics were corresponding.

The Figure -1 & Figure -2 depicts the handwritings of Taranjit Singh (After Incarnation) and the handwritings of Satnam Singh (Before Death), in Roman Script. The points of similarities have been duly marked in these figures.

For Instance,

1a. The letter "A" is written in three pen operations and its top is open in both the writings.

2a. The staff and curve of letter "B" is written separately in both the writings.

3a. The letter "C" has a shallow curve in both the writings.

4a. The letter "E" is written in four pen operations in both the writings.

5a. The junction of letter "G" is upward in bot the writings.

6a. The letter "O" has anticlockwise oval which joins at 11'o clock position in both the writings.

7a. The letter "N" has left down slant and angular base in both the writings.

8a. The letter "M" has angular retraced junction and right hand staff is longer in both the writings.

9a. The letter "L" has upward lower stroke in both the

writings.

10a. The letter "T" is written in two pen operations is both the writings.

11a. The letter "S" has lower short curve in both the writings.

12a. The left staff of letter "X" is longer than the right staff in both the writings.

13a. The letter "P" is written in two pen operations in both the writings.

14a. The letter "H" has been written in three pen operations

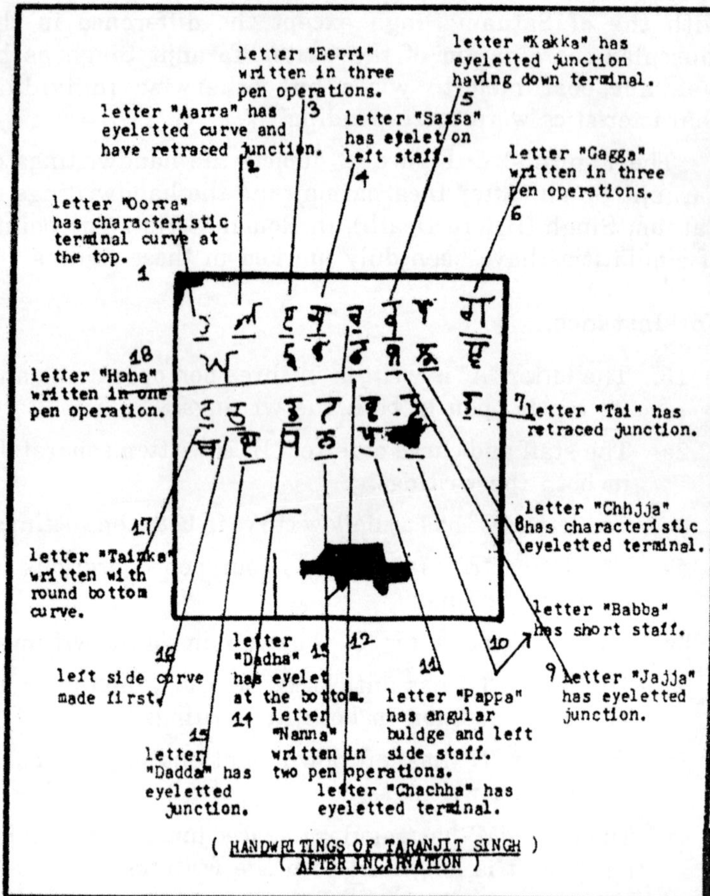

(HANDWRITINGS OF TARANJIT SINGH)
(AFTER INCARNATION)

Fig. 3

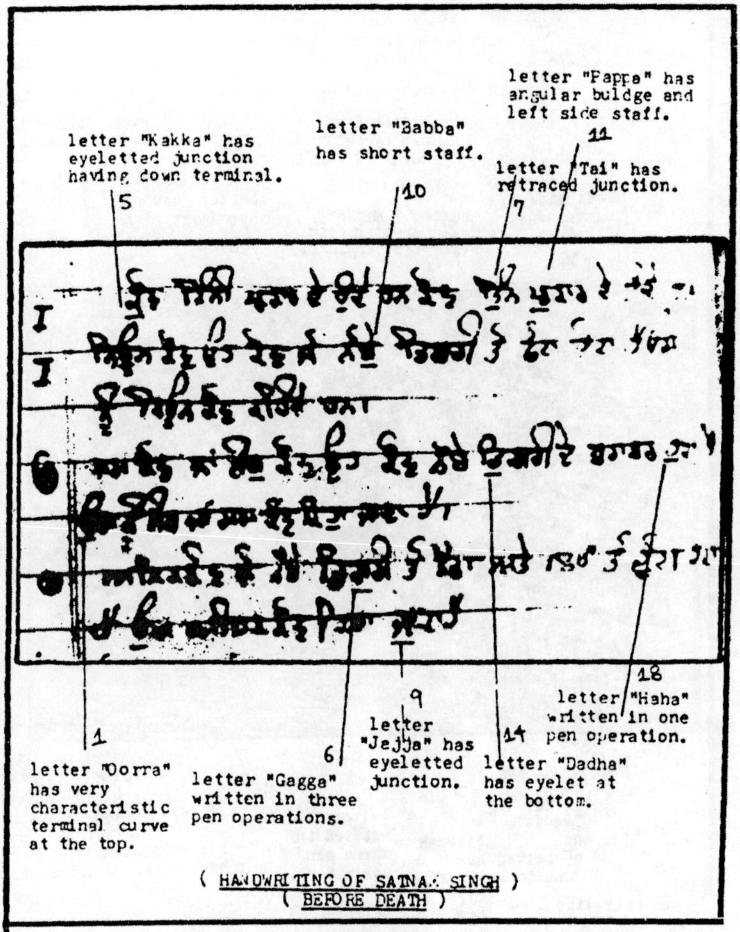

Fig. 4

in both the writings.

The Figure-3 and the Figures-4 & 5 depicts and handwritings of Taranjit Singh (After Incarnation) and the handwritings of Satnam Singh (Before Death), in Gurmukhi Script. The points of similarities have been duly marked in these figures.

For Instance

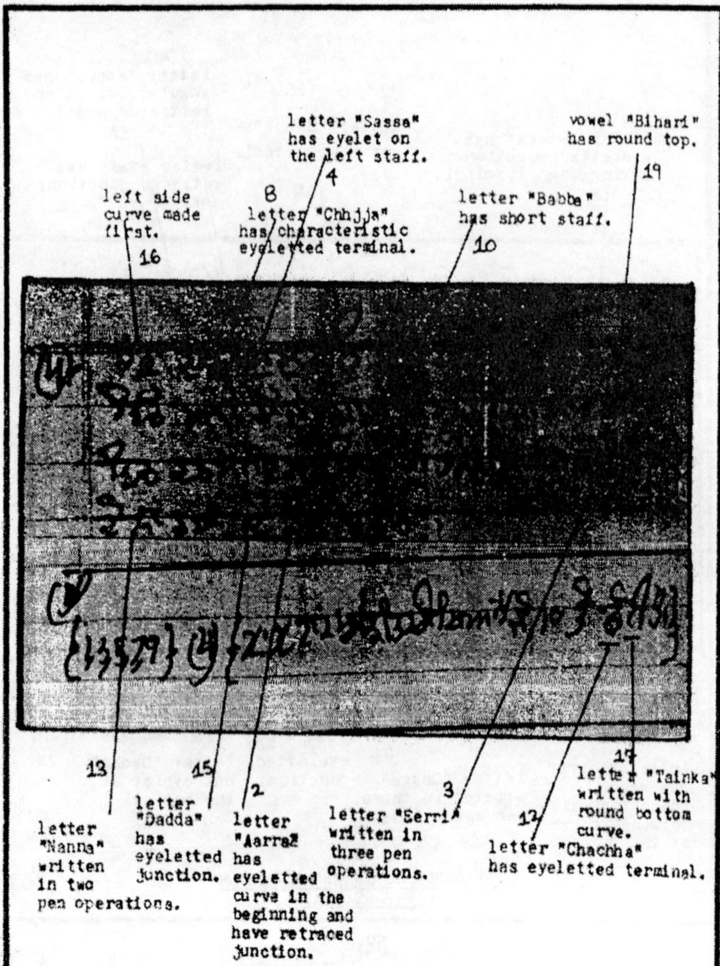

(HANDWRITINGS OF SATNAM SINGH
(BEFORE DEATH)

1. The letter "Oorra" has characteristic terminal curve at the top in both the sets of writings.
2. The letter "Aarra" has eyeleted first curve and have retraced junction in both the writings.
3. The letter "Eerri" has been written in three pen

operations in both the writings.

4. The letter "Sassa" has eyelet on the left staff and is written in three pen operations in both the writings.
5. The letter "Kakka" has eyeleted junction and having down terminal in both the writings.
6. The letter "Gagga" is written in three pen operations in both the writings.
7. The letter "Tai" has retraced junction in both the writings.
8. The letter "Chhjja" has characteristic eyeleted terminal in both the writings.
9. The letter "Jajja" has eyeleted junction in both the writings.
10. The letter "Babba" has a short staff in both the writings.
11. The letter "Pappa" has angular left bulge and left side staff in both the writings.
12. The letter "Chachha" has eyeleted terminal in both the writings.
13. The letter "Nanna" has been written in two pen operations in both the writings.
14. The letter "Dadha" has eyelet at the bottom in both the writings.
15. The letter "Dadda" has eyeleted junction in both the writings.
16. In the letter "Thatha" the left side curve is made first in both the writings.
17. The letter "Tainka" is written with round bottom curve in both the writings.
18. The letter "Haha" is written in one pen operation in both the writings.

Conclusion

It is clear on the basis of similarities in the individual characteristics between the handwritings of Taranjit Singh and Satnam Singh that the author of these handwritings is one and the same person.

If it is preseumed that the soul is transferred from one person to another then the mind will remain same. If soul of Satnam Singh (Who is dead) is believed to be transferred into the body of Taranjit Singh (Who is alive), the handwriting produced by Taranjit Singh will be corresponding with that of Satnam Singh, as in the present case.

Thus it has been proved scientifically on the basis of handwriting comparison that the departed soul of Satnam Singh has been transferred into Taranjit Singh and lived again.

REFERENCES

1. Bhaktivedanta Swami Prabhupada A.C.: *Coming Back, The Science of Reincarnation,* Bhaktivedanta Book Trust, Bombay, 1987.
2. James Greene & David Lewis: *Handwriting Analysis,* Treasure Press, London 1990.
3. Osborn, A.S.: *Questioned Documents,* Nelson Hall Co., Chicago, 1929.
4. Puri, Jagjit: *Selected Works of Dewan K.S. Puri on Disputed Handwriting and Finger Prints Comparison,* Dewan K.S. Puri Foundation, Patiala, 2001.